It Will Never Work

25 years of Urban Splash
1993 – 2018

Edited by
Miles Falkingham

Foreword by
Deyan Sudjic OBE

Contributions by
Michael Evamy
Mark Latham
Robert Senior
Tom Bloxham MBE
Jonathan Falkingham MBE

Documentary photography
Felix Mooneeram

Foreword
Deyan Sudjic OBE

Developers for the most part believed that nobody had ever gone bust by underestimating the taste of the British public.

The real point of reflection is to tell us something about what happens next, rather than to offer the consolations of living in the past. Looking back across a quarter of a century at the Britain of 1993 is to see a place that is both eerily familiar, and yet utterly different. It was the year that saw the first beginnings of many of the things that have made the country what it has become. Unemployment passed the psychologically troubling three million mark, a figure that suggested that the country was trapped in something more like a depression than a recession. John Major saw off the Maastricht rebels and UKIP was founded. James Dyson sold his first vacuum cleaner having mortgaged his house to pay for the tools needed to make it, and the legal bills to defend his copyrights. Irvine Welsh published Trainspotting. Disney opened up outside Paris; the first time that the mouse put wine on the menu. The Channel Tunnel was getting ready for public service. The Princess of Wales retired from public life. In a Liverpool still reeling from decades of decline and civic chaos, 1993 was the year that Derek Hatton the Trotskyite ex leader of the council was acquitted of corruption charges.

Two years earlier a bar opened in a previously run down part of Liverpool city centre. Baa Bar was characterised by a vivid orange and blue colour scheme and a pragmatic use of exposed structural props to create a striking façade for the expenditure of as little money as possible. It was the project that brought Tom Bloxham and Jonathan Falkingham together to form a new property company, called Urban Splash, that set out to convert redundant industrial and commercial spaces to residential use. Set against the kind of things that were going on in Barcelona still in its post Olympics glow, or dare it be said even Manchester with the Haçienda, it was not the first example of what would soon be described as hipster cool. But it was an early sign that something new was happening in a city that had not had much to feel good about since The Quarrymen set off on the road that would take John Lennon to Hamburg. (In fact the musical background to 1993 was a mix of Snoop Doggy Dogg, REM, Phil Collins, the Proclaimers, Radiohead and Nirvana).

The first Urban Splash development Concert Square suggested that the kind of ideas Jane Jacobs had been promoting about nurturing street life and the dangers of clearing so called slums ever since she had written The Life and Death of Great American Cities were finally beginning to have an impact in the North.

Deyan Sudjic OBE is a British writer and broadcaster, specialising in the fields of design & architecture. He is the director of the Design Museum, London. He was co-founder and editor of Blueprint and his most recent book The Language of Cities is published by Penguin.

New Islington Masterplan by Will Alsop, 2003

Park Hill, Sheffield, 2018

Look at Liverpool now, or Manchester, or Sheffield or Birmingham and they have turned into what seem like a different urban species. It's a change signalled by city centres filled with street life – for better, and sometimes for worse and by skylines punctured by picket lines of sharply sculpted, colour accentuated new towers. Unlike their less flamboyant concrete predecessors that they have come to overshadow, these are built for sale, or to house students, rather than to provide social housing. Urban Splash of course is not responsible for all of this, but it has played a significant and highly visible part not just in changing how cities look, but perhaps even more our preconceptions about them. And it has been responsible for many of Britain's most impressive projects outside London, from Plymouth's Royal William Yard, to the restoration of Birmingham's cylindrical office tower, the Rotunda. They have also commissioned a uniquely open minded range of architects. They gave FAT their only major project in Britain, built housing designed by Will Alsop as well as by Norman Foster.

In 1993 we knew for a fact that high rise social housing was a total and unmitigated disaster. We knew that the big cities outside London were rotting at their heart, those who could leave them were in full flight for suburbia or green satellite towns. Even London which had begun to see the doughnut effect, the hollowing out of its centre, go into reverse still had a million fewer citizens than in 1939.

Developers for the most part believed that nobody had ever gone bust by underestimating the taste of the British public. Dealing with old buildings was regarded as difficult to finance, and unnecessarily complicated. For most planners traditional zoning was still a key issue. Work had to be kept at a safe distance from home and play.

Lenders did not like the idea of funding offices that included retail or restaurant spaces at ground level, for fear of legal complexities.

Twenty-five years ago we saw the architecture of the recent past differently. In 1960 Ivor Smith's team of architects at the city council completed the Park Hill complex which has dominated Sheffield's skyline ever since. It was opened by the then leader of the Labour Party with high hopes for the transformative power of modernism. By 1993 it was considered among the most appalling examples of the welfare state forcing the poor to live in conditions of dangerous squalor. That was the year that the complex was the scene of a four hour stand-off between armed police and the occupants of one of the flats on its dilapidated streets in the sky. It wasn't just the siege that signalled the degraded nature of the development to those who were ready to use it as the justification for Mrs Thatcher's onslaught on public housing. It was the supposedly depraved condition of the surviving inhabitants. The local newspaper reported that a group of residents had set off a barrage of fire crackers in the hope of drawing the police into a shoot out for the purposes of their own entertainment. The place had a reputation long before that for damp, cockroach infestations, and crime. In 1979 there had been the tragic accidental death of an eight year old child, struck by a television set lobbed off one of the upper floor balconies. Not surprisingly, when the blocks were listed by English Heritage, the response in much of the city was of disbelief. One opinion poll suggested that far from being preserved as modern landmarks, 90 per cent of those answering would prefer to see them demolished. Look at it now, the most effective demonstration of the possible.

That Urban Splash should have the courage to take Park Hill on, and emerge through the financial crisis of 2008, to carry out a comprehensive transformation of the entire complex, maintaining its essential architectural and urban qualities, making 25 per cent of its refurbished flats available to the social sector, and persuade private buyers that this has become a desirable place to live is little short of miraculous. The comparison with what was possible in the much more financially benign climate of London where nobody had the appetite to save the perhaps even more impressive Robin Hood project, designed by Alison and Peter Smithson and demolished this year, is instructive.

Working with English Heritage, and joint architects Studio Egret West and Hawkins Brown, Urban Splash stripped the blocks back to a concrete core, and patched it up with the same attention to detail that the Society for the Protection of Ancient Buildings would have brought to restoring the sandstone gothic vaults of a cathedral. They also dared to inject colour into the grey concrete frames, using a bright palette applied to aluminium sheets built into the facades in tribute to Le Corbusier's paintwork at the Unite d'Habitation in Marseilles. It is a project that has transformed not only Sheffield but attitudes elsewhere about what development can be, and what design has to offer. It is also a vindication of what Urban Splash can accomplish. This was style put to work in the cause of substance.

By the time Urban Splash took on the resurrection of Park Hill, it had already set out on an equally radical and equally ambitious piece of urban renewal in east Manchester that required a different strategy. New Islington was a tabula rasa, a field of dereliction that had already seen two different incarnations wiped out in the course of 50 years. In the 1950s the industrial slums that had so horrified Marx's collaborator, Friedrich Engels when he wrote The Condition of the English Working Class had been flattened to make way for what quickly became new slums. Harnessing both public and private funds, Urban Splash used all the skills, techniques and attitudes that had driven it from a scrappy start up into the mainstream, to create a new identity for the place. New Islington was once called the Cardroom Estate which was not the stereotypical high rise slum, but made up of two storey terraced houses which still failed. The new name, chosen by popular ballot, was the first step in an attempt to transform the area and recreate a part of the city that had all but lost the will to live. It learned from three generations of mistakes to set about creating a new community the size of a small town.

Too many cities are made as the outcome of conventional formulas and unintended consequences. Urban Splash continues to show very persuasively that there will be better options.

Too many cities are made as the outcome of conventional formulas and unintended consequences. Urban Splash continues to show very persuasively that there will be better options.

Town House, Keeper's Quay, New Islington, 2016

Preface

Urban Splash are a property development business founded in 1993 by entrepreneur Tom Bloxham and architect Jonathan Falkingham. They profess to have started without a plan. The early model was one of opportunistic innovation, seeing and realising value others had overlooked. They were often told 'it will never work', this was invariably a call to action rather than a pause for thought.

Twenty five years on, Urban Splash have won over 50 RIBA Awards for design excellence, more than any other developer (as well as recognition in many other fields across regeneration, enterprise and marketing). The RIBA awards cross the spectrum from Small Projects to the Stirling Prize Shortlist and cover refurbishment and new build on residential, leisure and commercial schemes. Special awards acknowledge the company's commitment to Sustainability, Housing and Conservation.

It Will Never Work started life as an exhibition, co-curated by Urban Splash and Suzy Jones at RIBA North, exploring Urban Splash's award-winning projects in the context they were created and distilling the attitude and values that made them possible. The exhibition divided the story into blocks of time linked to significant social, political, economic and cultural events. The chapters in this book follow the same structure, and this goes some way to describing the specific projects in their context, and perhaps how this context helped the company to create, rather than react to, new futures.

This chronological approach tells us less about the underlying motivation or ethos that drove the business from challenge to challenge. Often these things are embedded in personality rather than written on paper. A series of 'provocations' throughout this book, and as giant lightboxes in the exhibition, represent core convictions that cut across the immediate context to form a common set of values and motivations. Of course the book and exhibition were conceived initially as a celebration of a significant milestone. It's something of an achievement, 25 years, more so because Urban Splash have emerged from such a testing time, with almost a decade spent dealing with the aftermath of the credit crunch. It very nearly didn't work, not in the end through the risky business of innovation but through the risky behaviour of financial markets.

So this is a story of the rise and fall and rise again. Big lessons have been learnt but chief amongst them was to follow core convictions, not to let short-term distortions of the market shape the business.

In telling this story the brief has been to tell it honestly, including a new commission to revisit past projects by photographer Felix Mooneeram. The photography in this book is in the main documentary rather than archival, a photographic record of how these projects look today rather than a back-catalogue of press shots. This is perhaps the best measure of the quality and durability of the projects and a truer picture of the Urban Splash legacy.

The final chapter is written by Urban Splash's Regeneration Director, Mark Latham. Dream on looks forward and sets out Urban Splash's priorities as they begin the next 25 years. As Deyan Sudjic writes so succinctly in his foreword: "The real point of reflection is to tell us something about what happens next, rather than to offer the consolations of living in the past."

About the editor: Miles Falkingham co-founded cross-disciplinary practice Shed and architectural practices shedkm and Union North. Miles is a designer, editor and curator and designed and co-curated the It Will Never Work exhibition.

It Will Never Work, Exhibition at RIBA North, 2018

RISKY BUSI- NESS

The approach to risk should include the certain knowledge that the stock response and the usual advice lead to more of the same. In business it is useful to know what worked in the past but essential to strive for what will work in the future. Innovation is always a risky business, but for a pioneering business playing it safe is a risk you can't afford.

Concert Square, Liverpool, 1993

Cities are bad
The early nineties

1991. Urban was a negative word – urban blight, urban deprivation, urban decay – but for Urban Splash cities were places of promise, urban was a word they were happy to adopt in their name – as a deliberate challenge and provocation.

In Manchester manufacturing has been eradicated from the city in the 1980s and the canals fell quiet years ago. After 5pm, the city centre dies. It's a brave person that walks these streets on their own after dark.

Manchester isn't alone. In cities across the north of England, warehouses and factory buildings litter city centres, the relics of industrial prosperity, now derelict and dangerous. Recession is biting, livelihoods are being lost. The national dole queue races towards three million. The dispatch of British bombers and troops to expel Saddam's troops from the oilfields of Kuwait does nothing to lighten the mood.

There are still bands, DJs and raves to keep young spirits up. But the Smiths have long gone and Madchester is not what it was. The Happy Mondays are partying in Barbados, and bankrupting Factory Records. A drugs-related police clampdown causes the Haçienda to temporarily close its doors.

At Affleck's Arcade, the traders are defiant. The red-brick former department store on Oldham Street is a stronghold of alternative culture. It's the place for fresh vinyl and baggy jeans. One of the stallholders is Tom Bloxham, who's wondering if he could make an Affleck's work somewhere else.

At Affleck's, Bloxham expands into posters, reprinting band photos and the foldouts that come with LPs, and selling them to students for a handy premium. It's an early lesson in adding value: turning the mundane into the must-have. But the poster sales are still not his number one income generator. He realises that sub-letting the space he doesn't need for his market stall brings in more than records and posters put together. Welcome to the property business.

He looks for a site where he can repeat the Affleck's Arcade model. In Liverpool Bloxham snaps up a clump of derelict Georgian warehouses for the price of a terraced house, and makes an indoor market from it, which he calls Liverpool Palace. Above the arcade of indie retailers on the ground floor are makeshift offices taken by designers, bands and entrepreneurs. It becomes a base for The La's, Wayne Hemingway and the founders of Cream, among many others.

Just around the corner, recently-qualified architect Jonathan Falkingham has just set up Shed, a cross-disciplinary design practice, with his brother Miles Falkingham. Unlike some of his fellow graduates who've sought out junior jobs in cities like Berlin and New York, Falkingham has stayed put. He believes his passion for architecture can make a difference in a Liverpool hit hard, like Manchester, by factory and port closures, and chronic unemployment.

In the middle of a recession, you need to create your own opportunities. Falkingham knows a number of Bloxham's tenants and gets wind of his plan to create a bar next to Liverpool Palace. He pays the entrepreneur a visit and asks if he has an architect. Bloxham shows him his own design, sketched out on a sheet of A4. Falkingham is told there's a budget of £70,000. When he offers to design it and to get it built for that sum, Bloxham accepts.

Shed delivers, creating an iconic bar, its furniture, fittings, lighting and even its name on a shoestring, stepping in to do some of the manual labour themselves to bring it in on budget. Baa Bar opens to rave reviews and front covers in the design and lifestyle press. It brings something unheard-of in north-west England: continental café culture. Coffee and the papers in the morning, tapas in the afternoon and DJs in the evening.

Bloxham is converted: design, done well, can create something new and entirely different. It can tell a different story about a street, a neighbourhood, and potentially a whole city – a story about renewal and reinvention, brought about by a fresh, ballsy, independent northern attitude.

PHOTOGRAPHS BY JONATHAN KEENAN

THE LIVERPOOL SCENE

Liverpool's warehouse district, where nineteenth-century commercial buildings line the maze of narrow streets that lead down to the docks, is currently undergoing sympathetic regeneration. Enthusiastically rechristened the "Creative Industries Quarter" by developers Charterhouse Estates, its current mix of small-scale artistic enterprises operating in studios, workshops and rehearsal spaces will stay, and students will be encouraged to occupy those buildings to be converted into flats as a low-cost, industrial approach is applied to rehabilitating the redundant warehousing.

All in all, this should provide a ready-made, local clientele for the Baa Bar, the designer watering hole that Liverpool never had in the 1980s. Here Shed, the young design team responsible for the interior, has achieved dramatic effects with the simplest of means and created a space that is hardwearing and uncluttered but visually stimulating. Unlikely objects are employed as functional decoration: isolators salvaged from an electricity sub-station are sandwiched between breeze blocks and extruded metal to form the bar; Tri-shaws (which usually support motorways under construction), span the glazed front and hold up the first floor; an eclectic range of light-fittings were found in local hardware shops and a high-street catalogue showroom.

Different spaces are defined using words and colours. The three letters of Baa are writ large in plywood down one wall and reflect the transparent spandex letters attached to the bar's glazed facade. The inviting reds, oranges and pinks of the bar area contrast with the clinical green light in the corridor that leads to the toilets. The exterior in industrial blue and orange is well suited to its surroundings.

The mix of materials and surface treatments results from the range of skills brought to the project by different members of the group. Jonathan Falkingham trained as an architect in Liverpool, and stayed. He set up Shed with his brother Miles, a fine artist who turned to graphic design when he saw the need in Liverpool for a practice that could come up with modern design solutions without charging the fees of a larger or London-based firm. A loose set-up also allows the brothers to bring in the most suitable freelance help for particular projects (they drafted in Colin Harwood on his return to Liverpool, after working on large-scale interior conversions for David Marks and Julia Barfield in London, to work with them on the Baa Bar) and provide a multi-disciplinary approach.

This flexibility has paid off. Shed are now working, in conjunction with the Ian Darby Partnership, on a rather larger interior project: the 051 nightclub. Housed in the basement of Liverpool's Media Centre, it should be finished early this month.
Liz Farrelly

PAST

28 October 1991 **Blueprint**

Baa Bar, Blueprint, 1991

JRES NEW

Concert Square, Liverpool, 1992

Concert Square, Liverpool, 1994

In Liverpool and Manchester's old industrial buildings, Bloxham and Falkingham see the bone structure for the kind of regeneration taking place in London's Docklands. Loft living has entered the British consciousness. An ad for Halifax Cardcash featuring an old Commodores track and a single guy with a cat makes the case for warehouse conversions everywhere.

Like their contemporaries, Bloxham and Falkingham are taking city breaks in Europe. The colour and 24-hour vitality of Paris, Rome, Barcelona and well-populated city centres is inspiring.

They picture disused factory floors as dream flats, and no-go areas as new neighbourhoods. High ceilings, huge windows, bare brick and space for all your friends. Places where creative people can gather, live and collaborate, with flexible, short-term leases, and shops, bars and workspaces. It's a blueprint for the mixed-use urban regeneration of the future.

Bloxham and Falkingham recognise a meeting of minds and a shared excitement about what might be possible in the neglected cities of north-west England. A business is formed. Their vision is captured in the name that Falkingham coins: Urban Splash. They just need the right building to give them a start.

Soon, a suitable site appears at the right price: a former chemical factory next to Liverpool Palace, one block back from Bold Street, one of Liverpool's major thoroughfares. Learning as they go about the planning process and other red tape, and relying solely on gut instinct to guide their decision-making, they set about transforming the building into Liverpool's first set of loft-living apartments.

Without hiring a main contractor, they count on labour they can find themselves to get the job done. They strip out the building, leave original brickwork exposed and marry the best of the old and the best of the new. At the front of the building they level the space to create Liverpool's first new public square in a century. It's the pair's first strategic and counterintuitive move.

Concert Square is seen by agents and the local property crowd as a crazy enterprise. Again and again, Bloxham and Falkingham are told, "It'll never work". Who'd want to live in a run-down part of central Liverpool when they can afford a nice semi with a garden out in the suburbs? We would, they say. And so do others. Concert Square fills up with Liverpool's coolest, inside and outside. Pavement café culture springs up in the square. Before long, the people who said it would never work are saying it's too busy.

The success of Concert Square confirms the pair's determination to ignore the market and silence doubters. By reinventing the space around the building and generating a buzz inside it, the development transforms preconceptions of its location.

It sets a template for the next projects at Ducie House and Smithfield: industrial buildings brought to life with judicious juxtapositions of old and new, with the presence to draw people like a magnet to overlooked parts of town. There's no conscious intention to subvert property industry norms, just a desire to keep finding new, challenging opportunities, to keep doing projects they believe in and that add to the cities they love, and to keep getting better at what they do. Plus, of course, a determination to prove the naysayers wrong.

The Urban Splash way is born.

The early nineties

Concert Square
Liverpool

Residential / Commercial / Leisure
Architects: Urban Splash Architects / Shed

It's hard to think back into the mindset that was around then. Today we think of cities positively, as drivers of growth and places where the good life can be lived. In hindsight it was as much belief and persistence as judgment that drove this project through when all the indicators where pointing the other way. A bit of luck, some skill, a lot of persistence.

Tom Bloxham

The first Urban Splash loft, Concert Square, Liverpool, 1994

Before 'placemaking' was a word I think we understood that a great location doesn't have to be a pre-existing condition. In our first project our first action was to give land away – not the norm for developers – to create a new public square and make a place where people would want to live.

Jonathan Falkingham

Kiosk, Concert Square, 1995

Smithfield Buildings
Manchester

Residential / Commercial / Leisure
Architects: Stephenson Bell Architects

Initially we didn't know there was an atrium. The strip out was like a giant game of pass the parcel, unwrapping a century of shop fits, one on top of the other, to reveal the original Victorian grandeur. As always the driver was to do interesting things, and do them well, not necessarily to do more or bigger. But our growing experience and scale increasingly allowed us to apply our ideas and ambitions and skills to larger and more complex projects, and Smithfield was a step up. We've continued to do that, moving from individual buildings to city blocks to whole neighbourhoods – the next generation of new towns?
We'd love to do that.

Jonathan Falkingham

Smithfield Buildings atrium, Manchester, 1996

Smithfield Buildings, Manchester, 2018

The ownership of the company has always remained private and that's allowed us to follow our gut when necessary. Investors and shareholders tend to want to repeat what's been done before. It has also allowed us to be agile in our decision making and seize opportunities – when we bought Smithfield Buildings the main tenant was bust, the owners were bust and the mortgage bank in possession were bust – and that was a time for gut feeling and decisive action.

Tom Bloxham

Smithfield Buildings, Manchester, 1996

Sally's Yard
Manchester

Residential
Architects: Urban Splash Architects

We were rolling out of the Haçienda at 4am when we found Sally's Yard. In the beginning there was no plan; when we saw an opportunity we went for it, and we knew then, as now, that opportunities usually present themselves as challenges.

To this day we're loath to let an exciting opportunity pass us by. Our recent acquisition of the modular housing division of SIG is a huge challenge and a huge opportunity.

Tom Bloxham

Manchester's first loft apartment, Sally's Yard, 1994

St Peter's Church
Liverpool

Commercial / Leisure
Architects: Urban Splash Architects / DK Architects

Artists are the vanguard of the urban revolution! From the beginning we've wanted to attract pioneering people to our projects, we have instinctively surrounded ourselves with creative, inventive and sometimes disruptive people. They make things happen.

Jonathan Falkingham

The crucifixion of St Peter by Norbert Attard, St Peter's Church, Liverpool, 2002

Pioneering urban living in the North West, Smithfield Buildings has been a catalyst for entrepreneurial and creative activity, attracting people to live in the area and locate new business.

Lord Richard Rogers,
Towards an Urban Renaissance
Urban Task Force

PUSH-
ERS &
JUNK-
IES

It's not all about bricks and mortar. Making successful places means understanding the value people bring, the role of artists as pioneers, the role of designers as facilitators and the role of every Tom, Vic and Hari in building a vibrant community. We should be enthusiastic art pushers and committed design junkies, because pioneering creatives will deliver intangible value to the places they inhabit.

Islington Square, New Islington, 2006 by FAT Architects

Cities are good
The millennium years

May Day 1997. A Labour landslide. Tony Blair is young, progressive and a symbol of a new confident, cosmopolitan Britain. A rosy glow envelops the nation.

Things really do only get better. Wales and Scotland get the devolution they crave. Peace comes to Northern Ireland. Britannia is cool. Britpop rules the charts. YBAs rule the RA (for three months, anyway). Wallpaper magazine and Grand Designs feed the appetite for domestic architecture and design.

In northern cities, councils with Labour majorities have the ear of central government. Lord Rogers' Reith Lectures for the BBC, titled Sustainable City, are adapted into a book, Cities for a Small Planet, which calls for a more European, city-centred style of living and spawns a wave of new thinking on urban regeneration.

Lord Rogers leads the Urban Task Force, which publishes Towards an Urban Renaissance. Smithfield Buildings is used as an exemplar of progressive, mixed-use city-centre regeneration. More than 100 recommendations include calls for design-led regeneration and more brownfield housing. The white paper catches the eye of No10, which sets up the Commission for Architecture and the Built Environment (CABE) to champion urbanism and building design as a 'public good' to sit alongside education and healthcare.

Nick Johnson, a long-time collaborator with Bloxham and Falkingham, and deputy chief executive at Urban Splash, becomes a CABE North West representative, bringing a refreshing dose of Mancunian savvy to the corridors of the London-based quango, along with a Liam Gallagher-inspired shaggy moptop and complicated anoraks.

Cities are the future. Regeneration projects receive generous injections of public funding through English Partnerships and other agencies. Lenders get the message and private investment follows. Credit easing means builders can build and buyers can buy. A tide of funding flows towards developments in previously untouchable urban neighbourhoods, unlocking major schemes across British cities.

Urban Splash is in the vanguard of the renaissance. The change of mindset towards urbanism and sustainable placemaking comes just as the company is hitting its stride, taking on larger, more ambitious projects.

Britannia Mills, Castlefield, 1998

Britannia Mills, Castlefield, 2000

Matchworks, Liverpool, 1998

Matchworks, Liverpool, 2001

Urban Splash's revival of the Tea Factory in Liverpool kick-starts the Ropewalks area regeneration. The conversion of a former match factory into offices will help turn the Speke Garston area of Liverpool into a lively business district.

A stream of open-plan loft apartments follow the early successes of Concert Square and Ducie House. Sally's Yard (in a Georgian warehouse), Britannia Mills (in a Victorian mill), Collegiate (in a neo-Gothic school) and Smithfield Buildings (in an Edwardian department store) all present their own challenges. In each case, the building's functional and aesthetic DNA is identified, reframed and celebrated to create a unique place to live. Original architecture is revealed and brought into contrast with contemporary new elements.

By the late 1990s, Bloxham, Falkingham and Johnson are thinking beyond interpretations of period architecture. They believe their approach can be transferred to new build homes, and that it could potentially provide a legitimate, contemporary, urban alternative to the faux-period box-like fare being offered by the volume housebuilders.

Never ones to merely dip their toe in the water, they test their theory by launching an architectural competition that attracts 160 entries and is decided by judges chaired by Lord Richard Rogers. An unashamedly modern design of glass and precast concrete is selected for the first major new build scheme by Urban Splash, at Timber Wharf, amid Castlefield's bleak post-industrial landscape. It proves to be a breakthrough project for a young Glenn Howells.

'Location, location, location' doesn't figure in the Urban Splash value system. Most of its projects continue to place a flag in the ground in areas where most property companies would fear to tread.

Overcoming entrenched negative perceptions and reversing long-term decline is achieved not just by creating homes. Its developments pay as much attention to the space around the building as to the building itself. The company becomes known for its placemaking: the creation of settings that encourage public activity and new uses, and of new identities for neighbourhoods that can signal change and optimism.

Meanwhile, Manchester has been awarded the 2002 Commonwealth Games. It's a major coup and a massive opportunity to display its resilience and imagination in the wake of the 1996 Arndale bombing. The city rises to the challenge.

While the London Eye, Tate Modern and the Millennium Dome rise in the capital, Manchester's shattered Cardroom Estate is identified as one of English Partnership's Millennium Communities. In 2002, Urban Splash is awarded lead developer status.

Will Alsop sketches the essence of the masterplan with a marker pen in one hand and a glass of good red in the other. One of the pivotal ideas is the linking of the Ashton and Rochdale canals, either side of the site, to bring the waterside into the heart of the development and offer a focus for community activity.

Residents select the uber-cool practice FAT (Fashion Architecture Taste) to design their new homes. Nick Johnson, Manchester born and bred, leads consultations with Cardroom residents, keeping them onside and discovering how they'd like to see their neighbourhood evolve, in official meetings and often over a pint afterwards.

New Islington starts to take shape.

The millennium years

Ropewalks
Liverpool

Residential / Commercial / Leisure
Architects: Urban Splash Architects / shedkm

Tea Factory, Ropewalks, 2018

The success of Concert Square had encouraged us to develop something of a 'campus' model – to continue building on that initial investment in placemaking at a city-block scale. The idea was not to simply replicate what had worked before – we've typically left that to others – but to keep adding organically to the proposition so that each new development enhanced the value of the whole. It's an overused phrase, but in urbanism the whole really does have to be greater than the sum of the parts – the whole being the neighbourhood, the quarter and the city itself.

Jonathan Falkingham

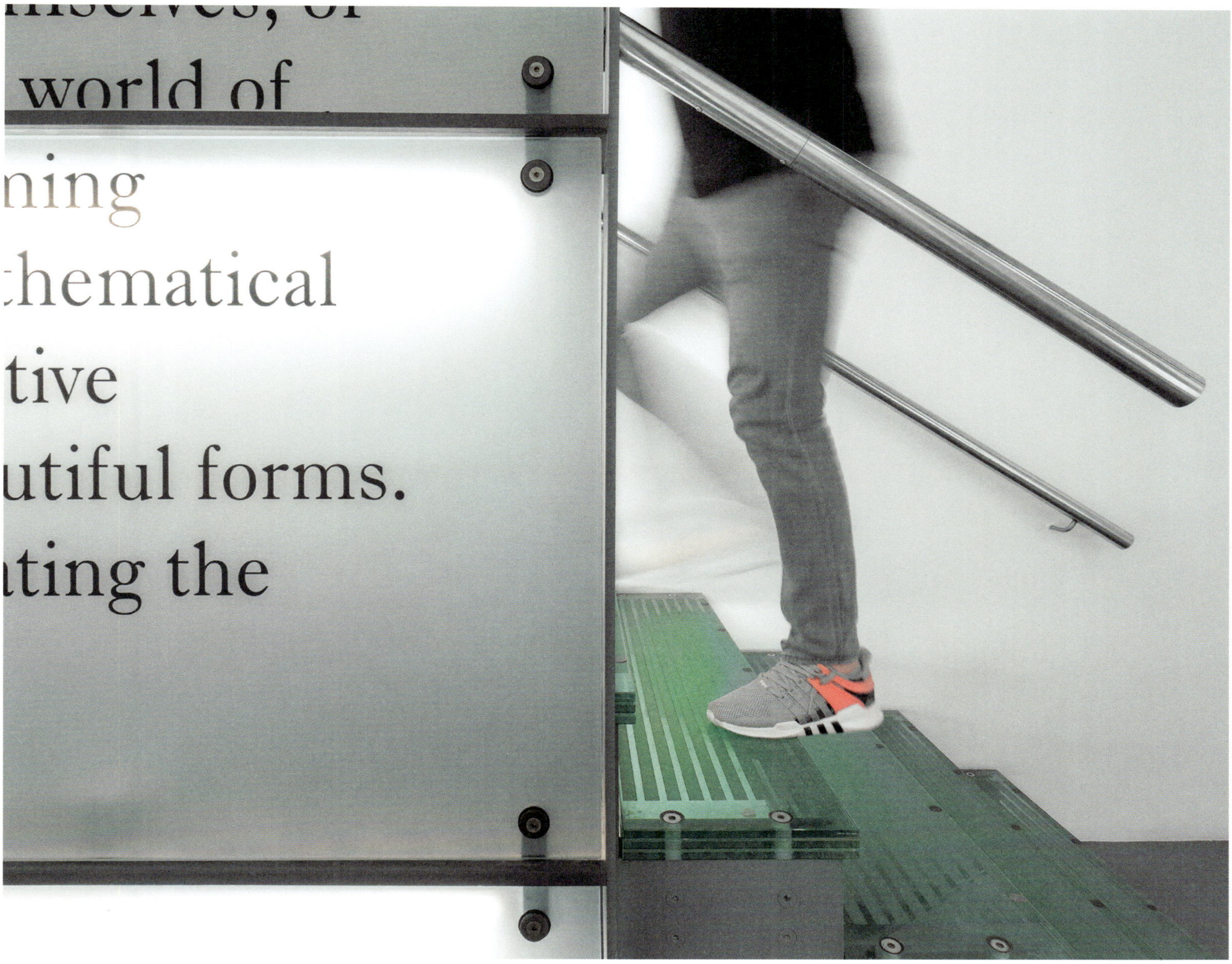

Main staircase, Tea Factory, 2018

Offices, Vanilla Factory, 2011

Mother Espresso, Tea Factory, 2018

Through projects like Matchworks and Ropewalks we were able to build up a very talented commercial team at Urban Splash. This extra string to our bow would prove critical later and still forms a very significant, but largely unsung, part of our success.

Tom Bloxham

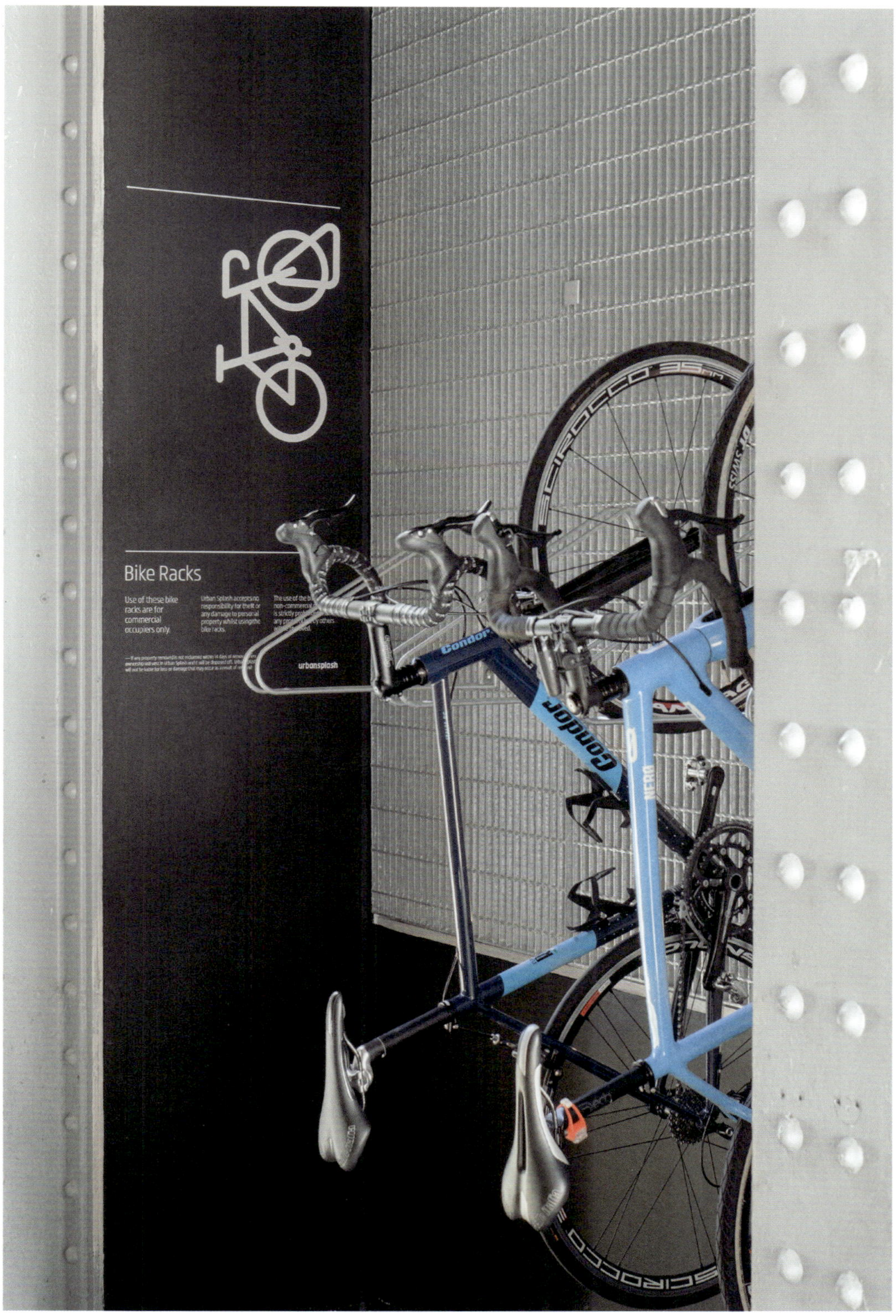

Tea Factory, Ropewalks, 2018

Office entrance, Tea Factory, 2018

concierge
Guild Energy
SPACES.
Cass Associates
Xposure Studios
SPACES.
SPACES.
JM RET
World Merit
3 Beat
Third Floor
301 SPACES.
302 The Campus
303 Cream Group
space@urbansplash.co.uk

Castlefield
Manchester

Residential / Commercial / Leisure
Architects: Urban Splash Architects / shedkm /
Glenn Howells Architects / Studio Maurice Shapiro

Beyond the inner ring road – the inner city – was a place that other developers feared to tread. The canal was key – while the ring road pushed us out the canal connected us back into the heart of the city. The challenge was considerable: we needed to create a new enclave from scratch and without repetition. Perhaps here and in New Islington the multi-authorship approach matured from instinctive to strategic. We were working with the best architects, engineers and artists to deliver variety and quality as well as scale.

Jonathan Falkingham

Britannia Mill and Burton Place, Manchester, 2018

Box Works, Manchester, 2018

Imitation is never a problem, if we're not inspiring imitators then we're following and not leading. The early city-centre developments had inspired a whole raft of imitators, big corporate players to fly-by-night chancers. We felt that the next challenge, and the next opportunity, lay elsewhere. The big idea was to turn an industrial area of sheds and redundant mills into a great place to live. Close enough to walk to the city centre but far enough away not to be kept awake at night by the ever expanding number of bars and restaurants in the city.

Tom Bloxham

Urban Splash head office, Timber Wharf, 2018

Box Works, Manchester, 2018

Moho courtyard, Castlefield, 2018

Urban Splash head office, Timber Wharf, 2018

Matchworks
Liverpool

Commercial
Original architects: Mewes and Davis, 1919
Architects: shedkm

It was a new adventure, we wanted to create a high-quality business park in a great Liverpool location populated by interesting businesses that would create lots of jobs. We applied the same methodology of simply designing fantastic spaces people wanted to be in. Whether you're living or working, loving the place is still massively important.

Jonathan Falkingham

Matchworks, Liverpool, 2018

Matchworks, Liverpool, 2018

Matchbox at Matchworks, Liverpool, 2018

My first visit was poignant – matchmaking equipment was still there but all the jobs had gone – I knew many people from my wife's family that had worked there. It was post-industrial Liverpool, once the countries biggest match works now closed. Perhaps with a bit of chutzpah we said we would create more jobs than had existed before and I'm proud to say that is what we have done.

Tom Bloxham

Matchworks, Liverpool, 2018

New Islington
Manchester

Residential / Commercial
Architects: dMFK Architects / FAT / shedkm / Mae / SMC Alsop / Stephenson Bell / Sixtwo Architects

Taking on the redevelopment of one of Manchester's worst estates was always going to be a challenge. The bones of the plan came from a sketch by Alsop. It was an opportunity to extend our placemaking skills, creating Manchester City Centre's first new park, a new marina with residential moorings, a new health centre, we sponsored a new Free School. We worked with great architects, Will Alsop, FAT, dMFK, Mae and Stephenson's and brought in other developers large and small, who shared our ambition.

Tom Bloxham

Cotton Field Park, New Islington, 2018

Cotton Field Park, New Islington, 2018

Town House, New Islington, 2018

The great thing about our appointment as lead developer was that it was based on reputation rather than a masterplan. This meant we could conduct true and meaningful consultation with the existing community and not impose a pre-approved plan. Positivity was everything. We wanted to raise expectations and encourage the local community to see the energy and creativity of our team as a way to achieve something exceptional, that truly reflected their values as well as ours.

Jonathan Falkingham

Town House, New Islington, 2018

Alsop's masterplan for Urban Splash in New Islington, gives space for FAT and the residents to create houses that plunder the canons of high architecture and our everyday popular culture.

Alex Mowat,
Building Design,
April 2006

GOLD DIG- GERS

It is the property sector's devotion to spreadsheets that razes good buildings to the ground, overlooks poorer neighbourhoods and delivers replicants not exemplars. We need to dig deeper, looking for value others have missed and along the way change perceptions of places and save buildings destined for the wrecking ball.

Melville, Royal William Yard, 2017

The bad and the ugly
The noughties

With the economy thriving, Chancellor Gordon Brown declares the end of boom-and-bust. Wages are rising, unemployment is falling. Car sales reach their highest-ever level.

For the first time, Manchester is being regarded as the UK's second city. The destruction wrought by a 3300lb bomb at the city's Arndale Centre in June 1996 has provided the springboard for swathes of the city centre to be improved, remodelled and rebuilt. Manchester City Council has actively encouraged a 24-hour economy and pavement-bar culture to make the centre a safer, more liveable place.

The Metrolink tram and local rail network is branching out into the suburbs. The new City of Manchester Stadium hosts the 2002 Commonwealth Games, which accelerate regeneration of the east of the city. Manchester seems poised to fulfil its potential; 'The B of the Bang', the daring sculpture by Thomas Heatherwick for the games, seems to speak for the city as well as for world-beating sprinters on the starting blocks.

At its new HQ at Timber Wharf, Castlefield, Urban Splash is thriving and expanding rapidly. With more than 100 property and design awards under its belt, its portfolio continues to grow. Urban regeneration has become a highly bankable opportunity. Credit is easy to come by, for investors big and small. A new generation of homebuyers are moving into the former factories and warehouses where their parents and grandparents spent their working lives. The urban renaissance is well and truly under way.

Like the floorboards and brickwork in a typical warehouse development, the template for creating loft-living apartments has now been laid bare for all to see. Developers eyes light up as the potential value of converted industrial architecture in downtrodden locations starts to dawn. The surge in credit brings a host of Urban Splash imitators, all putting forward their own versions of the genre in regeneration zones across the north-west. Some good, with real attention to quality, community and placemaking, some not so good.

The bandwagon is rolling. The competition for historic city-centre mills and warehouses becomes fierce, and their price climbs accordingly – tenfold in some parts of the region. At Urban Splash, the loft-living market is not the opportunity it once was. Its natural impulse is to seek out new problems to solve: new build developments, and other categories of historic building in more challenging locations that can stretch its problem-solving and value-adding faculties.

Midland Hotel, Morecambe, 2006

Midland Hotel, Morecambe, 2009

The company spreads its wings, geographically and typologically. Major new build schemes such as Budenberg HAUS Projekte in Altrincham, designed by Foster + Partners, join signature revivals of period buildings in 'difficult' locations, such as Lister Mills in riot-troubled Bradford, the imposing stone storehouses of Royal William Yard in Plymouth and the faded art deco Midland Hotel on Morecambe's seafront.

Journalists start talking about the apparently Midas-like 'Urban Splash effect'. The company is sought out as regeneration partner of choice by councils across the country, the go-to guys for buildings and projects no one else will touch.

The company's appetite for a challenge only seems to grow. It takes on the 'bad' buildings, the so-called 'problem projects' that no one knows what to do with. Langworthy estate in Salford is a neighbourhood of run-down, two-up, two-down Victorian terraces earmarked for demolition, and requiring complete reinvention as Chimney Pot Park. The huge, decaying remains of the Fort Dunlop tyre factory on the M6 present a seemingly insurmountable task of renewal.

It tackles the supposedly 'ugly' ones, as well – unloved, almost taboo, building types. Birmingham's Rotunda is the cylindrical office block on top of the Bullring, and – although listed – a white elephant with no takers. Park Hill, also listed, is a sea of notorious 1960s slab blocks, looming over Sheffield – a mammoth, long-term project of physical and social renewal.

A trio of unloved ex-council tower blocks on the edge of Manchester city centre is given new life and renamed after the Pankhursts, the city's suffragette sisters, following a public naming competition.

In Leeds, a pair of 1960s council blocks is reinvented as Saxton, a green urban oasis, with six and a half acres of gardens and allotments.

Burned-out and stigmatised these buildings may be, but they are still structurally sound, with great views across their respective cities, and the space available for communal gardens and greenery. With fresh facades, floor-to-ceiling glazing and open-plan interiors, eyesores become eye-catchers, bringing affordability for homebuyers and reversing decades of decline for urban neighbourhoods.

The phone keeps ringing with intriguing and tempting new propositions. The company recruits a new cohort of directors and staff, opening up regional offices in Yorkshire, the Midlands and the South-West in the process.

The challenges, and the commitments, are growing. And the housing market is heating up. There is no shortage of lenders and investors willing to put cash into Urban Splash schemes, but the money comes with strings attached. Pre-sales are a precondition of many loans, and buy-to-let purchasers begin to exert their influence on the size, mix and layout of units, driven by spreadsheet formulae and investment yield optimisation. For these buyers qualitative design considerations and the 'Would I live there?' test are not part of the equation.

Nevertheless, by 2008, the company has been flying high for 15 years. It is turning over £100m a year. It has 2000 apartments in the pipeline, with the next two years' production all presold.

The noughties

Royal William Yard
Plymouth

Residential / Commercial / Leisure
Original architects: Sir John Rennie Jnr, 1826
Architects: Ferguson Mann Architects /
Gillespie Yunnie Architects

Challenges usually arrive with a phone call. 'We have a problem building...' are words that often herald an unscripted diversion ahead. Plymouth was not in our plan and Royal William Yard was the wrong side of a port city on its uppers, historically like many docks it had a red light district on its doorstep. It was clearly an architectural gem but the sheer scale of the site would have been a challenge to even to the most audacious developer. But challenges are what we live for and some opportunities simply can't be passed by.

Tom Bloxham

Mills Bakery, Royal William Yard, 2018

Slaughterhouse, Royal William Yard, 2018

Royal William Yard, Plymouth, 2018

RIVER

South West Peninsula Coast Path, Royal William Yard, 2018

Brewhouse, Royal William Yard, 2008

Mills Bakery, Royal William Yard, 2018

We knew that attracting new business to animate the dockside was key, we approached every restaurateur in the City and none dared take a unit, ultimately the passion of our commercial team won through, first one independent business then many more. We love independents, they share our pioneering spirit and where the independents go others usually follow.

Jonathan Falkingham

Midland Hotel
Morecambe

Hotel / Leisure
Original architects: Oliver Hill, 1933
Architects: Union North

Many of the places we transformed have been unloved or unknown. We took pride in uncovering value in buildings that had been overlooked. The Midland Hotel was altogether different – our first public consultation was attended by 3,000 people. We were aware, of course, of its architectural significance but that meeting brought home to us that this building really mattered. It had become a barometer of the town's fortunes and spoke of past glories and of terminal decline. To bring this building back to life was regeneration at its most vital.

Jonathan Falkingham

Sun terrace, Midland Hotel, 2009

Restored elevation, Midland Hotel, 2009

Morecambe suffered a long decline, firstly as a fashionable resort and later as a popular seaside town – its customers dwindled as Yorkshire weavers and Scottish miners suffered large scale closures and overseas holidays and flights became ever cheaper. Morecambe responded (wrongly in my view) by building attractions like Frontier Land and Mr Blobby Land. But it could never compete with nearby Blackpool. The real attraction was staring us in the face, the amazing coastline and the wonderful but decrepit Midland Hotel. In many towns and cities it is hard to know where to start – here it was obvious – The Midland.

Tom Bloxham

Restored Eric Gill relief, Midland Hotel, 2009

Grand central staircase, Midland Hotel, 2009

Rotunda
Birmingham

Residential
Original architects: James Roberts, 1965
Architects: Glenn Howells Architects

We always start by asking, 'Would I live or work here?' Yes or no make for easy decisions. More often it's maybe – if I could arrive in style and enjoy the panoramic views with floor-to-ceiling windows... The belief that we're not that different to everyone else becomes the basis of the brief; it's not what we think other people would accept but what we would accept for ourselves.

Jonathan Falkingham

Rotunda, Birmingham, 2008

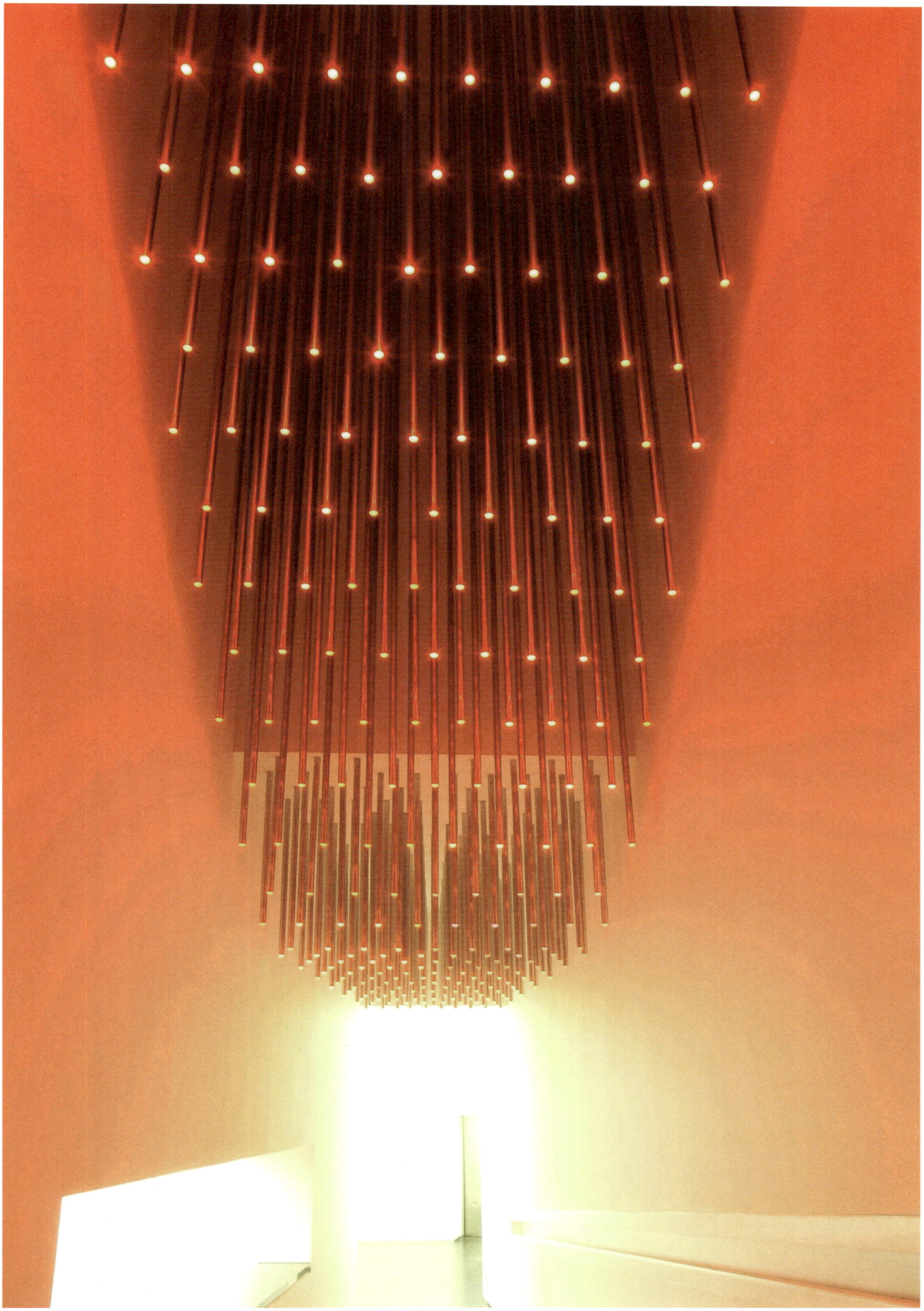

Residential lobby, Rotunda, 2008

3Towers
Manchester

Residential
Architects: Union North

Tower blocks (especially 1960s concrete ones) have an awful reputation in the UK and if towers were bad, these were bad towers in a 'bad' neighbourhood. But where others can't see beyond the negatives we like to dig a little deeper. With many first-time buyers already priced out of city centres was there salvation on the fringe? Could we deliver affordability, diversity, amenity and proximity – and in a fabulous elevated position overlooking the Irk Valley and City Centre.

Tom Bloxham

Emmeline, 3Towers, 2009

Emmeline, 3Towers, 2018

3Towers, Manchester, 2009

Chimney Pot Park
Salford

Residential
Architects: shedkm

Most houses were 'tinned up' others were being sold for less than £10,000 in the back of pubs to the worst type of private landlords, everyone was in negative equity and couldn't get mortgages. We were told there is no demand for Victorian two-up two-down terraces – we questioned this – they sold for £200k in Didsbury and £2-3 million in Mayfair (called Mews!).

Tom Bloxham

Chimney Pot Park, Salford, 2018

First floor garden, Chimney Pot Park, 2018

Chimney Pot Park, Salford, 2018

If we are not solving a problem we are not innovating. In Housing Market Renewal areas, traditional terraced houses in traditionally working class areas were considered part of the problem not part of the solution. But to us the idea that the terraced house had passed its sell-by date was ludicrous. In the end people queued for two days to buy the first of our 350 terraced houses, which had previously been earmarked for clearance.

Jonathan Falkingham

Lister Mills
Bradford

Residential / Commercial / Leisure
Original architects: Andrews and Pepper, 1873
Architects: Latham Architects /
David Morley Architects / shedkm

Challenging buildings come in all shapes and sizes, but most have simply been caught out by history – buildings whose purpose, location or rationale has been superseded. The scale and wider significance of Lister Mills (as with Royal William Yard and others) led us into a close working partnership with the local authorities, regeneration and conservation bodies. The partnering skills learnt on these projects would prove crucial in the years to follow.

Jonathan Falkingham

Rooftop Pods, Lister Mills, 2018

Silk Warehouse, Lister Mills, 2018

The first time I saw this I was bowled over by the scale and ambition of Samuel Lister, inventor and entrepreneur, who built it in 1873. Lister Mills had been neglected and unloved for almost 40 years, we knew we had to bring it back to life.

Tom Bloxham

Lister Mills, Bradford, 2000

This is about how we convert what have been liabilities in the past to what will be assets in the future.

John Prescott,
Deputy Prime Minister,
June 2003

Self Promoters

Robert Senior

At 25 Urban Splash has not lost its impulse to communicate with its audience at an eye to eye level, as if to a friend rather than to a prospect.

Buildings and marketing have more in common than one might imagine. They both last longer when they are well constructed, and they both leave lasting impressions when they capture the imagination through their aesthetic. Beyond the physical, buildings and marketing are both based on storytelling. Not just having a story, but telling it well. And when the story captures the essential truth and heartbeat of a brand, it works. Urban Splash celebrates a quarter of a century of colourful, provocative and brilliant storytelling. Is this a 21st Century marketing masterclass? Quite possibly, but in reality its marketing simply told the Urban Splash story as the chapters unfolded – look closely and you'll find no marketing artifice, rather you'll find a window into the soul of the company and its founders, Tom Bloxham and Jonathan Falkingham.

Tom and Jonathan have steered the company through a number of distinct phases of brand development, each punctuated with a particular attitude and behaviours. At launch Urban Splash was a shameless, iconoclastic up start, zigging pugnaciously to the zag of the norm. A proud challenger brand, they wore the clothing (and in Tom's case the hats) of dissent with pride. The next phase was of an established and respected grown up start up, having outgrown the old clothes. Then 2008 happened. Like many businesses the era of post Lehman Brothers austerity forced a pragmatic approach to toughing out tough times. Today as Urban Splash celebrates its 25th birthday, it finds itself entering the category of thought leader, never having wavered from its original beliefs and values but having evolved to remain a thoroughly modern brand. Urban Splash is as much an online publishing platform as it is a world class creative property developer.

At 25 Urban Splash has not lost its impulse to communicate with its audience at an eye to eye level, as if to a friend rather than to a prospect. Perhaps at the heart of its success is the courage to imagine beyond existing conventions, daring to dream of a better way of living. And never forgetting the marketing maxim that reason leads to conclusions while emotion leads to action. And make no mistake, Urban Splash is in the action business. To quote Pink Floyd, 'it's louder than words this thing that we do'.

Robert Senior was founding partner of Fallon London and is the former CEO Worldwide of Saatchi & Saatchi.

Awkward squad

Project print, 1995–2008

In a world where everything was A4 and filing cabinets were king we wanted to stand out – literally. We introduced a standard print format that just wouldn't fit anywhere and if it was too good to put in the bin we reckoned it would stay out and proud not filed away.

Jonathan Falkingham

Actual size

The hard sell
Smithfield Buildings 1995

Most developers thought the word luxury in a swirly font was a magic spell. Where they marketed to a target demographic we spoke to people who were probably a bit like us. We designed print we liked and talked about the things that were important to us. In the process we produced brochures that were more about places and ideas than bricks and mortar.

Tom Bloxham

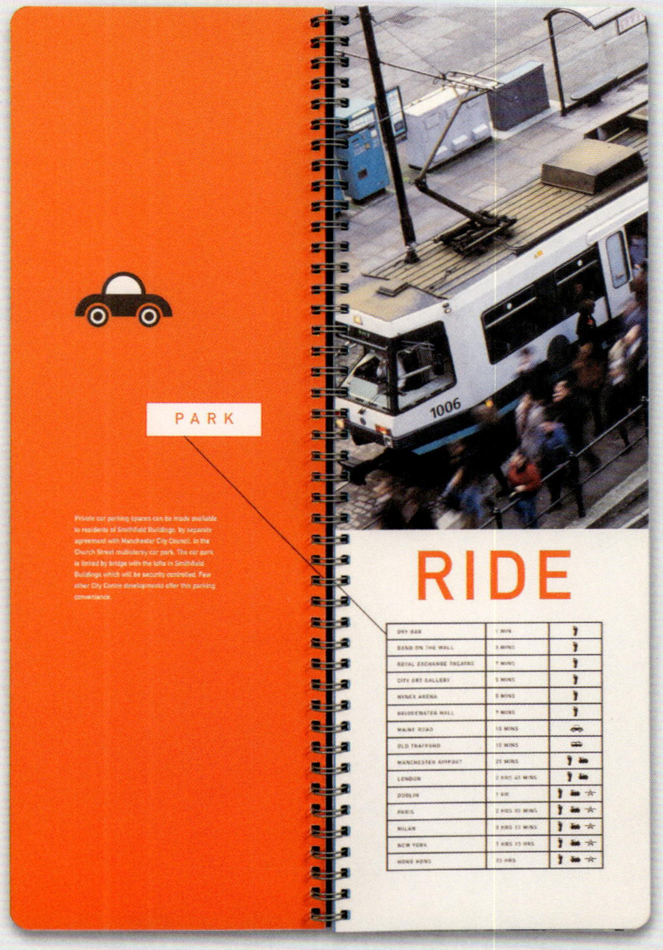

One size fits all
Project print, 1995–2008

Our format was our only rule, we worked with the best young designers in the cities they knew, their brief was to let the character of the place and the city shine through. Working with young designers, often from the arts and music sectors, was part of our celebration of all things creative, vigorous and urban.

Jonathan Falkingham

US.
URBAN SPLASH
THE BOX WORKS
SAXTON

Material world
Various projects

Because designers want to play and we didn't want to stop them.

Tom Bloxham

A VIEW OF LAKE SHORE,
BRISTOL

Sorry, not sorry
Chips, New Islington 2007

Of course having set some very basic rules, naughty Nick Johnson wouldn't stick to them. This is what happens when you fill your business with restless innovators.

Jonathan Falkingham

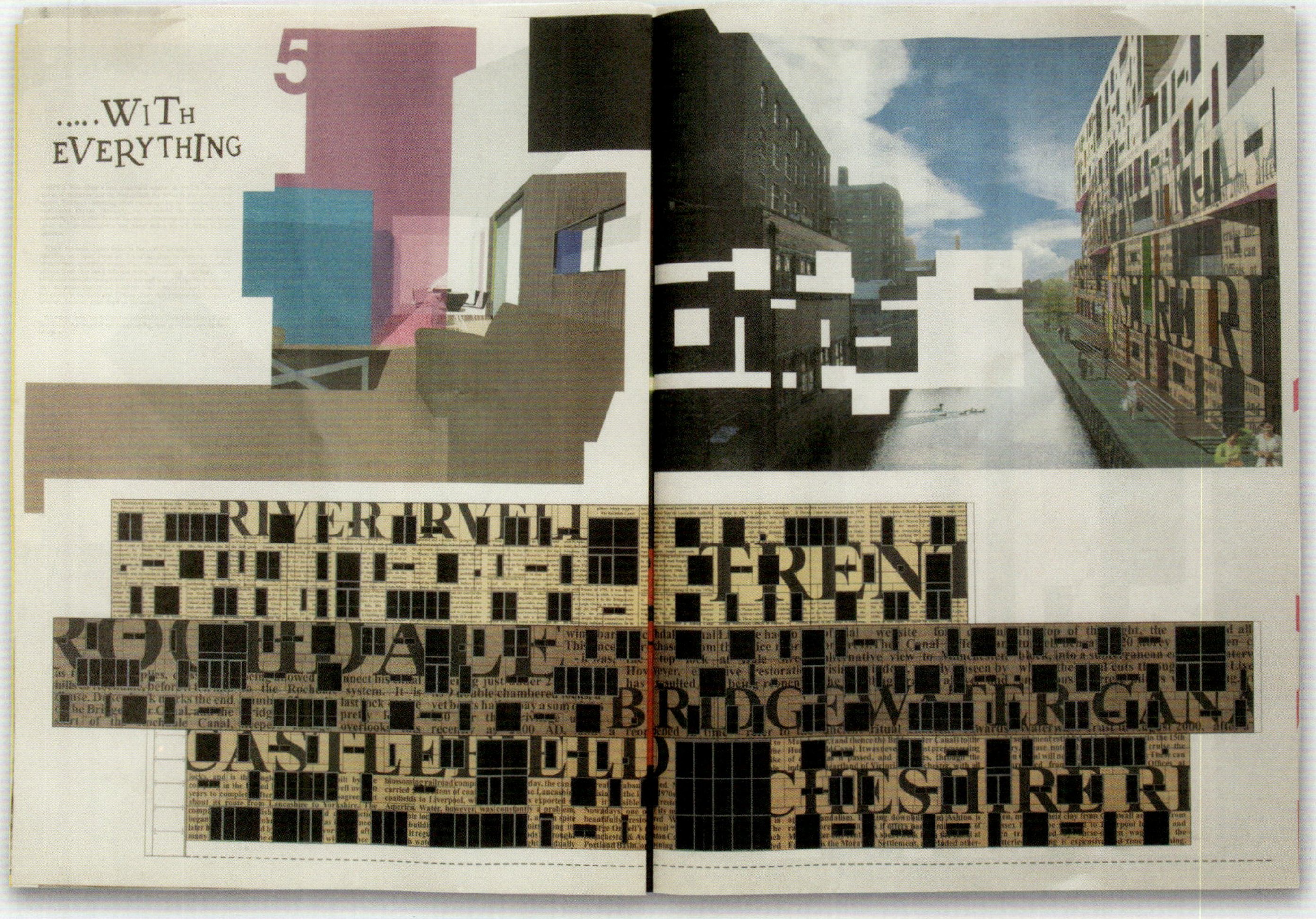
5
....WITH
EVERYTHING

Multi-media

Of course it's not just about print, although print has a habit of sticking around on shelves and in archives. Along the way we have commissioned animation, events, gnomes, cows, model boats and much more. A big part of our brand DNA is about having fun along the way.

Tom Bloxham

Digital Animation, Chips, 2005

Digital Animation, Rotunda, 2006

Rebrand 2008
North

As the scale of the business grew so control of the creative process became less direct and as this growth became more geographically widespread the brand needed to be more recognisable. This bold and simple rebrand put into words what we were thinking and into place some ground rules. The rule-breakers rule book.

Orla McGrath,
Urban Splash Marketing Director

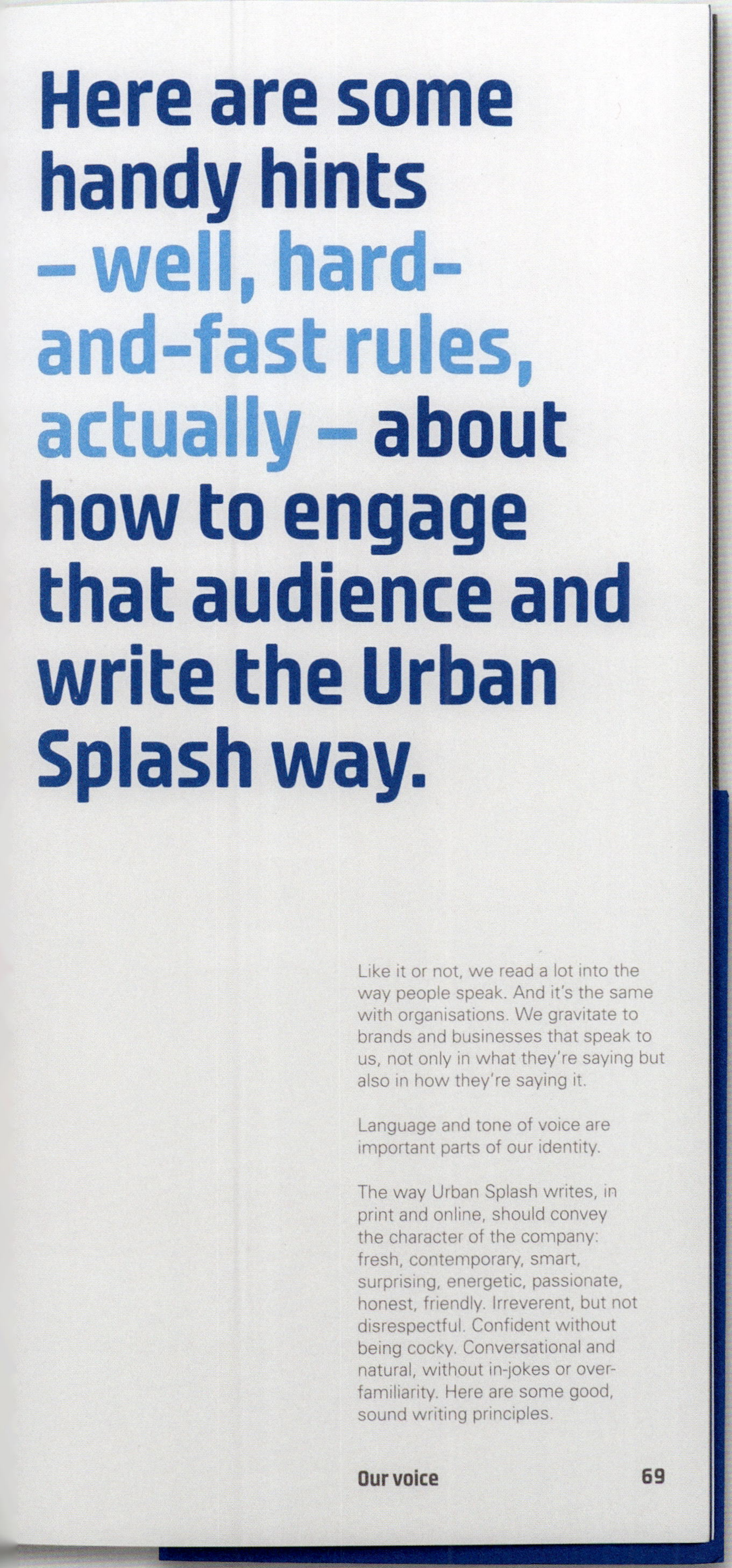

Here are some handy hints – well, hard-and-fast rules, actually – about how to engage that audience and write the Urban Splash way.

Like it or not, we read a lot into the way people speak. And it's the same with organisations. We gravitate to brands and businesses that speak to us, not only in what they're saying but also in how they're saying it.

Language and tone of voice are important parts of our identity.

The way Urban Splash writes, in print and online, should convey the character of the company: fresh, contemporary, smart, surprising, energetic, passionate, honest, friendly. Irreverent, but not disrespectful. Confident without being cocky. Conversational and natural, without in-jokes or over-familiarity. Here are some good, sound writing principles.

Our voice 69

Transformation

The contribution of Urban Splash to making the past work for the present is inestimable; Transformation should be on the desk of everyone with an interest in urban futures.

Sir Neil Cossons, 2012

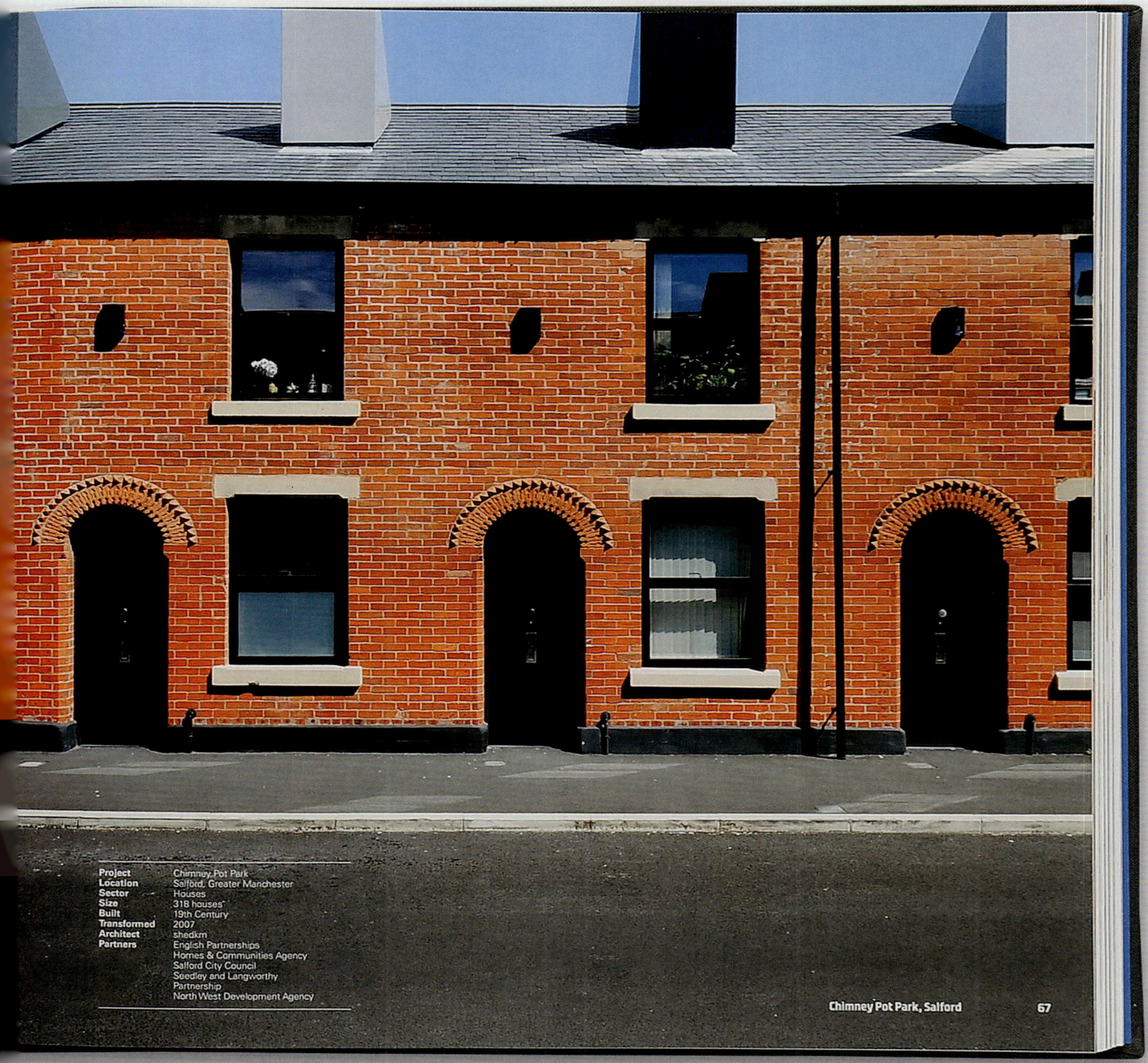
Project
Chimney Pot Park
Location
Salford, Greater Manchester
Sector
Houses
Size
318 houses
Built
19th Century
Transformed
2007
Architect
shedkm
Partners
English Partnerships
Homes & Communities Agency
Salford City Council
Seedley and Langworthy
Partnership
North West Development Agency
Chimney Pot Park, Salford
67

Arty business

We've always had an aversion to the kind of art that is placed on a plinth as a planning obligation. We don't need telling to be keen commissioners and supporters, we see artists as fellow innovators and we see art projects and artworks as an integral part of community – they should add to the sense of place, to the enjoyment and engagement in the spaces people share.

Jonathan Falkingham

Squiggly Wiggly the Giant Squid by Mordavaga, Royal William Yard, 2018

Bird House by United Creatives, New Islington, 2009

The Brutalist Playground by Assemble and Simon Terrill, Park Hill, 2016

18 DAYS OF
ART AND
16th June
YORKSHIREFESTIVAL.CO.UK

Illuminate Light Festival, Royal William Yard, 2017

RWY Ferry
Royal William Yard
Welcome

Brand refresh 2018
Smiling Wolf

We have a lot to show and not as much to prove – the earliest brand was full of design chutzpah and the latest is full of great content. The rebrand is designed to let the content be king – to allow us to talk about what matters and to let the projects speak for themselves.

Orla McGrath

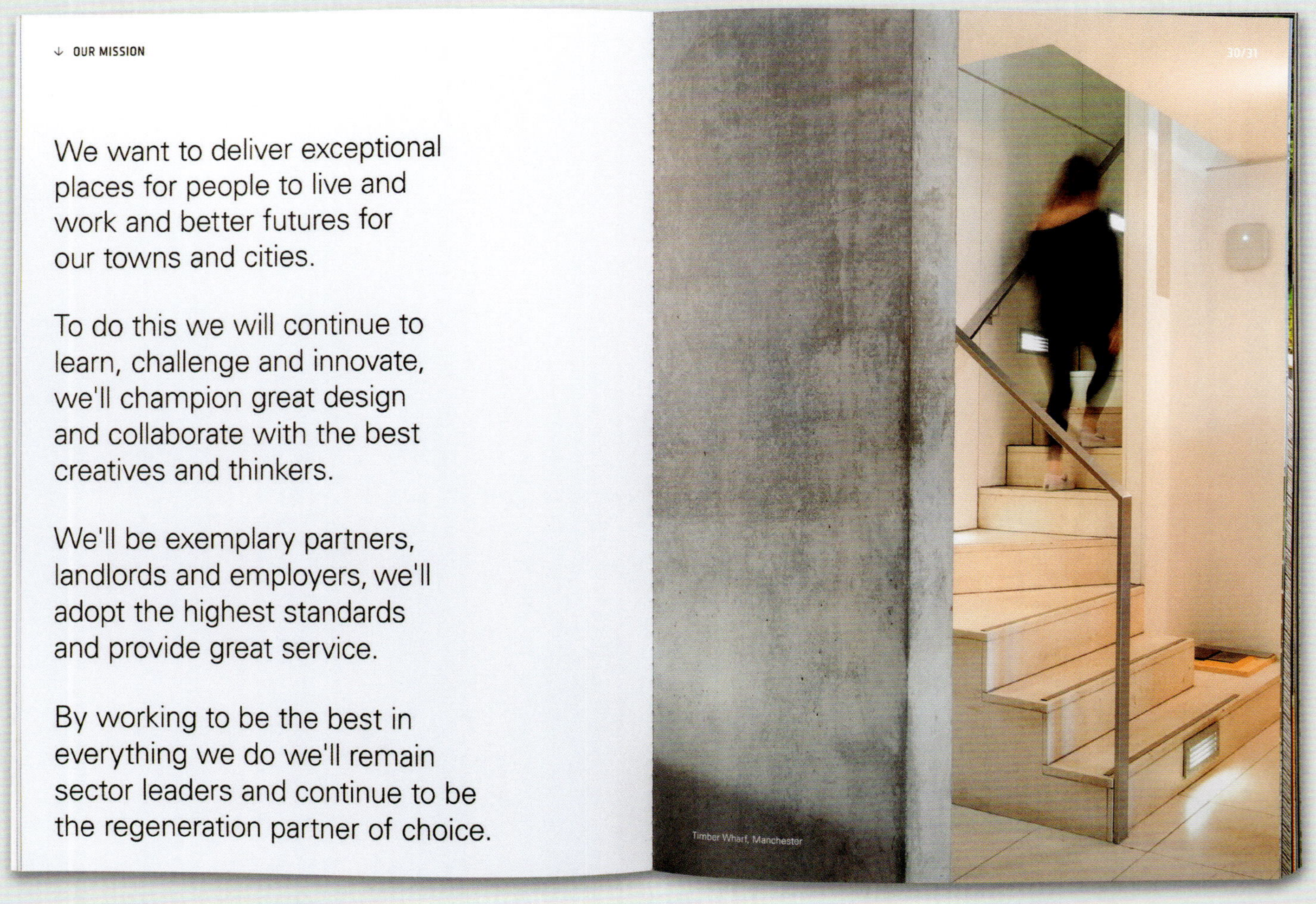

↓ WHAT WE WANT TO TALK ABOUT

62/63

Urbanism/Placemaking/
Transformations/
Great design/People/
City building/Collaborations/
Future neighbourhoods/
Iconic buildings/New ideas

↓ OUR KEY MESSAGES

32/33

01.
Rethinking
our cities

Cities are made of people and places. We began with small projects that encouraged pioneering people and transformed forgotten places. We've moved from individual buildings to city blocks to future neighbourhoods but our focus has remained on creating better places for people.

Park Hill, Sheffield

↓ SECTION 02
28/29
Where we're going
30 – 31
Our mission
32 – 61
Our key messages
62 – 63
What we want to talk about
We want to talk about the future –
it's where we're going.

Splash leads, you lot follow.

Tom Dyckhoff,
The Guardian

SUPER-
HUMAN

Planners, developers and architects should go beyond the minimum requirements and deliver exceptional places where real people want to live and work. Places we would live and work ourselves. We should always return to the idea that what we do at our best is the creation of the best possible human habitat.

What doesn't kill you
The crunch and after

2008. The year starts well. With a new logo and brand identity, even its own typeface, Urban Splash is sitting pretty, the poster-boy of urban regeneration.

The company makes the 2009 Cool Brands round up alongside Aston Martin, Jimmy Choo and Tate. But the subprime mortgage crisis in the US is spreading concern. The Urban Splash board, while wary of a potential downturn, have taken what feels like sensible precautions. With 80% of their development pipeline pre-sold, they will rent the rest and sit tight.

Then, on 15 September, Lehman Brothers collapses. Global economic meltdown follows. No one is prepared. No one is safe.

Overnight, the shutters come down on finance. Work stops on building sites across the country. Developers of a similar size to Urban Splash go to the wall. The company has major borrowings committed to big projects in Manchester, Sheffield, Leeds and Bristol. Buyers of apartments are pulling out in their dozens. Banks with whom it had signed long-term loan agreements are now on the phone, wanting their money back.

It is, in the words of Bloxham's beloved Sir Alex Ferguson, squeaky bum time.

A strategy is developed. The company halts work on all but a handful of key projects. In just a few weeks, expenditure on live projects nationally is slashed, from £10m per month to £1m. Many suppliers' contracts have to be terminated, but all are paid in full in the end, without any litigation. The ambition of developing a chain of boutique hotels, starting with Midland Hotel, is shelved, along with other non-core activities.

The Urban Splash payroll at the time of the crash stands at around 275. Uniquely for a property company, it employs in-house specialists to coordinate every facet of the development process, from deal-making and vision-forming through design and construction to sales, marketing and property management. It's a legacy of the company's earliest, most wet-behind-the-ears days, when it needed expert and trusted personnel on its side, full-time.

In the wake of the crash, with many projects at a standstill, the company has no option but to shed most of its staff. It shrinks dramatically and painfully, from 275 employees to just 75.

Opposite: Work in progress, Saxton, 2008

Lakeshore, Bristol, 2005

Lakeshore, Bristol, 2018

The company focuses on the projects that reflect its core strength: high-quality apartment schemes using contemporary design and sustainable placemaking, backed up by astute management of its retained commercial and residential portfolios.

It manages to raise £50m, in the teeth of the crisis, to complete key schemes. Saxton in Leeds, Albert Mill in Manchester, Lakeshore in Bristol and the first phase of Park Hill in Sheffield achieve some sales, but most of the new apartments are rented. Urban Splash becomes a landlord to hundreds of tenants, and a debt manager, working with accountants and lawyers to reduce the £250m of debt spread across the business.

It's a grind. Every Monday morning for two years there's a meeting with the company solicitor and accountant to check whether the company is a going concern for the next seven days.

While their peers are throwing in the keys, Bloxham, Falkingham and their co-directors are determined to continue. Pride in what they have built up over the last 15 years prevents them from doing anything else.

A restructuring of its debt in a major joint venture with property manager and developer Places for People, is crucial in helping to build a stronger business. Places for People, a former housing association, has been building an investment portfolio by buying residential stock. And Urban Splash has unsold residential stock coming out of its ears.

An initial sale of 800 units is agreed, but Urban Splash will continue to market and manage the stock. Places for People recognises the value of the Urban Splash brand in selling property to young homebuyers in the north-west.

The relationship flourishes. Both companies look to the other for support in completing tricky legacy projects. Their interests dovetail, and a development joint venture is established. Places for People offers financial muscle and a balance sheet to die for, capable of qualifying the joint venture for major bids. Urban Splash, meanwhile, has a track record and multi-disciplinary, cradle-to-grave skillset that allows the critique of potential projects from every possible angle, and that can't be found anywhere else. Most crucially, there's a meeting of minds: Places for People wants to become more adventurous in its approach to development, and Urban Splash has no intention of stopping, broke or not.

With years of hard work, invention and sheer bloody-mindedness, Urban Splash trades its way through the recession. The strength of its partnerships with local authorities and regeneration agencies, and the depth of its commitment to good design, pay off.

In late 2011, the RIBA publishes Transformation, a retrospective of the company's track record to date of bringing about physical and social change.

The company that was born in a recession comes of age in another one that's much, much worse.

The crunch and after

Fort Dunlop
Birmingham

Commercial / Leisure / Hotel
Original architects: Sidney Stott and W.W. Gibbings, 1917
Architects: shedkm

The derelict Fort Dunlop was an unmistakable landmark from the M6, it had become a very visible advertisement for the decline of manufacturing in the Midlands. With half a million square feet and no obvious use, turning this industrial monument into a symbol of regeneration would require more than great design – it needed advocates, collaborators, patrons and partners. The 'Urban Splash effect' was in large part the ability of our team to mobilise people around a vision. At Fort Dunlop as with many of our buildings the success of the project hinged on the belief and energetic participation of a great many people.

Tom Bloxham

Fort Dunlop, Birmingham, 2008

Fort Dunlop and the wider commercial portfolio was our salvation in some ways, the half a million square feet that had been such a daunting prospect, became a reliable source of income for the business when residential sales dried up. The earlier diversification and the diligent work of the commercial team saved our bacon.

Jonathan Falkingham

Office reception, Fort Dunlop, 2008

Rooftop terrace, Fort Dunlop, 2008

Saxton
Leeds

Residential
Architects: Union North

For us hard times meant back to basics. Survival meant outperforming the market, not by sacrificing quality but by redoubling efforts to deliver places where people wanted to live. Saxton was one of our most popular projects, with 410 homes delivered right in the eye of the storm. We proved that quality of place could generate demand where the wider market had all but evaporated.

Jonathan Falkingham

Allotments, Saxton, 2018

Saxton, Leeds, 2018

Saxton, Leeds, 2018

We had a problem and so did our banks – we needed a plan. The plan was simple – build out the buildings, complete them, sell what we can and rent the rest – we built up what is now called a 'private rented portfolio' of 800 homes. We raised in the depth of the crisis around £50m from HCA and HSBC and went to work.

Tom Bloxham

Saxton, Leeds, 2018

Longlands
Stalybridge

Residential / Commercial / Leisure
Architects: Space Craft

Longlands, Stalybridge, 2011

The credit crunch meant that existing development finance arrangements collapsed almost overnight – it was an extremely risky time. Longlands was one of several projects we continued to move forward when the whole sector had ground to a halt. The strength of our record, portfolio and relationships all helped us find a way to keep delivering, even in areas where values had been challenging before the credit crunch.

Tom Bloxham

Lakeshore
Bristol

Residential
Original architects: Skidmore, Owings & Merrill and Yorke Rosenberg Mardall, 1975
Architects: Ferguson Mann Architects

The enduring qualities of Lakeshore had to rise above the circumstances of its making. Behind the scenes there were furious efforts to keep the wheels on, but all to get us to where we needed to go. Even in difficult times we have to hold doggedly to what we know to be important, to support the architect in their vision and to deliver an exceptional place to live.

Tom Bloxham

Lakeshore, Bristol, 2018

Lakeshore, Bristol, 2018

Lakeshore, Bristol, 2018

Chips
Manchester

Residential / Commercial / Leisure
Architects: SMC Alsop

There are many more ways of living and varied family structures than there are conventional housing formats. Will Alsop wanted to get away from the standard series of small rooms, so folding screens replaced walls to give occupiers the freedom to define how they used space and to change it at will. Ideas like this are further developed in later phases at New Islington so that taken together they offer true flexibility, which encourages both social diversity and community resilience.

Jonathan Falkingham

Chips on completion, New Islington, 2009

Chips, New Islington, 2018

Matchbox
Liverpool

Commercial / Leisure
Architects: shedkm

We have always invested in design and looked to work with the best practices. We create opportunities wherever we can, this commercial pavilion at Matchworks was a beautifully executed new building that was a clear statement of intent for the wider project.

Jonathan Falkingham

Matchbox, Liverpool, 2018

I’ve lived in other apartments before, but Saxton is something completely different, it has a real sense of community. Being a stone’s throw from all the shops and restaurants, and yet having this huge outdoor green space, and my own allotment, is quite simply the good life.

Sarah Greene,
Resident at Saxton Garden

SCHEM-
ERS &
DREAM-
ERS

All planners, architects and developers should start with the belief that there is a better way, that change is opportunity and every new project should be an exemplar. It is the belief in better that will make us open to new ideas, intent on learning, enthusiastic collaborators and perennial dreamers.

Park Hill, Sheffield, 2018

How we live now
The twenty-tens

The global recession is over but austerity continues to bite. There are protests across the country at the depth and speed of public spending cuts, and their impact on the poorest in society.

The divide between north and south is widening. They are almost separate countries, says The Economist, such are the gaps in life expectancy, political leanings and economic trends.

Aware that austerity will probably make matters even worse, and that the sense of alienation in the north needs to be countered, Chancellor George Osborne outlines his vision of the 'Northern Powerhouse'. The promise is to rebalance the UK economy away from the capital. It includes improvements to transport connectivity, investment in science and innovation, and devolution of powers to elected mayors.

Great news. But back in the real world, static wages, rising prices and housing shortages leave first-time homebuyers miles behind. Millennials become Generation Rent.

The issue of affordability hasn't escaped Urban Splash. While the company's hatches are battened down during the recession years, it has been quietly working out how to disrupt the received wisdoms and standard practices of the volume housing market. The focus is on what makes people really love the places they live and work.

The company is eyeing the new build housing sector as ripe for a rethink. The standard volume-builder product is mediocre and dispiriting, based on small rooms, low ceilings and tiny windows. Ruthless cost control and vast supply chains make for a highly efficient business model maximising PLC shareholder value, but also a less than rewarding customer experience. Urban Splash believes there's an alternative.

In the meantime, a labour of love has been making progress. When Lehman Brothers crashed in 2008, work on the first phase of the Park Hill Estate renovation in Sheffield froze. The building's stripped-back concrete skeleton loomed over the city, a prophetic and inescapable symbol of the lean times to come, and of admirable intentions thwarted. Possibly.

To get the project even this far has been a feat of hard graft, diplomacy, patience and perseverance. Work finally resumes on the first phase, and in 2013, Park Hill is shortlisted for the RIBA Stirling Prize – the first Urban Splash scheme to be nominated for the UK architecture's highest accolade.

Park Hill, Sheffield, 2006

Park Hill, Sheffield, 2016

Through bold design and generous landscaping, and a fully pepper-potted, multi-tenure housing mix providing 40% of the flats at affordable rates, Park Hill attracts the highest number of owner-occupiers of any Urban Splash scheme to date. People of all ages and incomes add to the palpable sense of community.

Instrumental in the placemaking is the Urban Splash Commercial team, which introduces dozens of independent and creative businesses at Park Hill to complete the picture with a 'high street' of local services, shops, bars and cafés at ground level. Unlike many developers, the company refuses to leave commercial spaces on mixed-use schemes to the market, perhaps to sit empty for years to come. Park Hill becomes an emblem of hope and transformation, and of what can happen when great design, placemaking and community engagement take the lead.

Back at base in Manchester, thoughts have been turning to modular construction as a means of offering quality of design, choice, affordability and space, while remaining competitive with volume housebuilders on cost.

At New Islington, Manchester's Millennium Community, Urban Splash has planning consents for high-density apartment buildings. But these are no longer viable. It is pencilled in as the possible site for the company's first new build houses.

With continued R&D, the concept of House emerges. It's about reinventing the new build family home with quality and attention to detail. Giving buyers more of a say in the final product and specification, as they would when buying a car. Creating new, low-rise, urban neighbourhoods where public space, community and sustainability have been built into the thinking from the outset.

It's about space, light, contemporary design and the way we live now.

Urban Splash develops prototypes and delivers its first Town House community at New Islington in 2016. As usual, the test is, 'Would I live there?'. In early 2018, Urban Splash announces the purchase of its modular construction partner SIG, based in the East Midlands, and a full-scale commitment to the modular housing business.

Now as developer and manufacturer, they explore the development of a family of housing formats to meet the needs of different markets and locations. The typologies under development include Row House, a terrace-style product with a narrower footprint than Town House, and Mansion House, based on Victorian mansion blocks with a common front door and two apartments per floor.

House schemes are completed or under way at Irwell Riverside in Salford, Smith's Dock in North Shields and Port Loop in Birmingham. The challenge ahead is to scale up production and the size of House schemes, to drive economies of scale and bring prices down.

The company's eye is on the future – on the way we want to live our lives, both inside our homes and outside, and our relationship to the community and the local environment.

At Port Loop, a neighbourhood is being created for life in the 21st century. A manifesto is drawn up, sketching out how architecture, landscaping, design and services will satisfy future homebuyers' demand for play, for exercise, for green streets, for a subscription lifestyle, for low-carbon consumption, and for interaction with local like-minds.

The drive within the company and its leadership is as fierce as ever: to take on the big property and lifestyle challenges of the day, lead from the front and never to accept the status quo.

Who said it'll never work?

The twenty-tens

Royal William Yard Phase 2
Plymouth

Residential / Commercial / Leisure / Hotel
Architects: Ferguson Mann Architects / Gillespie Yunnie Architects

We take a long term view on all our projects. Some are completed and handed over, many more are a perennial work in progress. Eighteen years on, our truly dedicated commercial team are still working hard to add to and enhance the proposition at RWY. Along the way, we've created first a pioneering outpost, then a cool enclave and now a major destination. A big part of this process is about facilitating others – pioneering independents, upstarts and mavericks. Without them, it's just space.

Jonathan Falkingham

Ocean Studios, Factory Cooperage, 2018

The Column Bakehouse, Factory Cooperage, 2018

Factory Cooperage, Royal William Yard, 2018

Factory Cooperage, Royal William Yard, 2018

Stubbs Mill
Manchester

Commercial
Architects: Sixtwo Architects

We have become a house builder as well as a developer. We're delivering new neighbourhoods from scratch in the North East, the Midlands and the South. But when we see a great warehouse space underused and on our patch we simply can't resist. It's really not our core business anymore but it's in our DNA.

Tom Bloxham

Stubbs Mill, Manchester, 2018

Stubbs Mill, Manchester, 2016

Smith's Dock
North Shields

Residential
Architects: shedkm / SimpsonHaugh / George Clarke / TDO Architecture / Fabrik

Town House, The Plateau, Smith's Dock, 2017

In the depths of recession, we formed a new strategic partnership with Places for People, it was a means to an end but also the beginning of a great partnership. Working with Places for People we are delivering new neighbourhoods across the country, there is more ambition on all sides. It's a serious endeavour, and with genuine transformative zeal, we want to shake up the orthodoxy of identikit homes rolled out acre by acre.

Jonathan Falkingham

Town House, The Plateau, Smith's Dock, 2017

Town House, The Plateau, Smith's Dock, 2017

Fab House, Smith's Dock, 2018

Fab House, Smith's Dock, 2018

Fab House, Smith's Dock, 2018

Park Hill
Sheffield

Residential / Commercial / Leisure
Original architects: Jack Lynn and Ivor Smith, 1970
Architects: Hawkins Brown / Studio Egret West /
Mikhail Riches / Grant Associates

We loved Park Hill from the start, the decay was skin deep, to us much of the original ethos remained valid, it was a failure of management rather than vision. There was a complex balancing act between preservation and reanimation but original architect Ivor Smith was a firm advocate for our proposals, his aim had always been to create decent homes for people and he sensed the same passion and intent in our approach. I think we got the balance right, Park Hill graced the cover of English Heritage's 2009 Constructive Conservation in Practice, but more importantly it filled up with tenants and businesses who simply love the building for both it's historic and modern qualities.

Jonathan Falkingham

Park Hill, Sheffield, 2018

Aerial view Phase 1 complete, Park Hill, 2018

Park Hill, Sheffield, 2018

Park Hill was synonymous with urban decay and a poster boy for the failure of social housing experiments. To many in Sheffield it was a blot on the landscape and a stain on the cities reputation. While the Listing recognised it as an architecturally significant building, the Chief Executive of English Heritage was told listing Park Hill would mean 'it would never work' as housing.

Tom Bloxham

Park Hill, Sheffield, 2018

Park Hill, Sheffield, 2018

I think the Park Hill scheme gives real meaning to the word 'regeneration'; it represents a new beginning, a new vitality. I sense in those who have been involved the same enthusiasm and excitement that Jack Lynn and I enjoyed half a century ago. It will be a great place to live!

Ivor Smith,
original architect Park Hill

DREAM ON

When we talk about future neighbourhoods we should not be ashamed to sound a bit evangelical – there's not enough of it about. Too much mediocrity rolled out acre by acre. Not enough thought, not enough ambition. We are on the cusp of revolutions in personal transport, modular housing and flexible working – we should be in the vanguard.

Future garden city, Campbell Park North

Dream on
The future

Mark Latham

This book has told the story of our first 25 years. The ups, the downs, the successes and the mistakes, and the transformation, by us and others, of the urban landscape that Tom Bloxham and Jonathan Falkingham first saw as their playground back in 1993.

So much for the past. What of the future? What's on the Urban Splash drawing board?

Opportunism is in our blood, so we're not going to stop snapping up buildings full of potential and digging for gold. We'll always find it hard to resist the temptation of the occasional, one-off, eye-catching 'problem' project that others avoid or overlook, recently we didn't resist Civic in Plymouth, Boat Shed in Salford and Avro or Beehive Mill in Manchester.

And we'll continue to evolve and invest in our existing portfolio of properties and places. We'll go on refreshing and upgrading the commercial properties that have been a cornerstone of Urban Splash's success since the very earliest days, and we'll strive to extend, enrich and sustain larger, long-term, multi-phase projects as they mature into reborn neighbourhoods. Many of these projects have required years of stamina, patience and incremental (sometimes stop-start) progress, and remain among our proudest achievements. Ropewalks, Park Hill, Royal William Yard, Lister Mills, New Islington and Lakeshore have all been high on our priority list in 2018.

But as we move into our second quarter century there are two particular themes that, although they've been on our minds from day one, are taking up more and more of our attention and interest: the future of homes and the future of neighbourhoods.

Since we set about turning our first derelict factory into flats we've been questioning and challenging pre-conceived notions of housing markets and typologies. We started in the city centres of the post-industrial north, moved on to abandoned and shunned ex-local authority towers, slab blocks and brutalist estates, and re-purposed the back-to-back terraces of yesteryear with Chimney Pot Park's 'upside-down' homes. Do things have to stay as they've always been? We don't think so.

Mark Latham is Regeneration Director at Urban Splash

Future homes

Factory-built, affordable, flexible, beautiful.

We're determined to rethink and disrupt the tired formulas of the volume-building industry. The unswerving and ruthlessly efficient commitment to maximising shareholder value by minimising space standards. The penny-pinching on every brick course. The inch-by-inch shrinkage of window dimensions and floor-to-ceiling heights. The lowest-common-denominator rehashed styling and only-just-good-enough materials. Not only is the quality of the end product questionable, but the way homes are built has barely advanced in decades.

Our vision is for a different, better way of creating contemporary family housing. More space, higher ceilings, bigger windows. The ability to specify your own internal layouts and number of rooms, and the choice of living at ground-level or on upper floors (garden or loft-living). A crisp, contemporary, designer idiom that looks like it was made in the 21st century (because it was), rather than some pale pastiche of Victorian, Edwardian or interwar architecture. The quality control that comes with off-site construction in a warm, dry factory and transfer to site on low-loaders, ready-made and weatherproof. And all for a build cost that can compete with the biggest volume-builders.

Back in the depths of the recession, we initiated a major programme of R&D, design prototyping and proof-of-product work with long-term collaborators shedkm architects to create our first challenger house-type, Town House. Totally prefabricated, Town House rolled out of the factory and onto our site for the first time at New Islington in east Manchester, followed by sites on Tyneside and Salford. More projects are in the pipeline in Birmingham, Milton Keynes and elsewhere, and while the total volume of units produced to date is still in the hundreds. Town House has already had a major impact, winning numerous awards.

Town House

Fab House

We aim to offer what the market doesn't provide and perhaps what many buyers don't know they want. An unashamedly modern house, less cellular, with more light and more space. Another driver is the ability to bespoke specify the home, have more say in the final product and more options in how to live. But it's just as much about the space around our houses and the way it is used. We think there's a revolution on the way.

Jonathan Falkingham

Mansion House

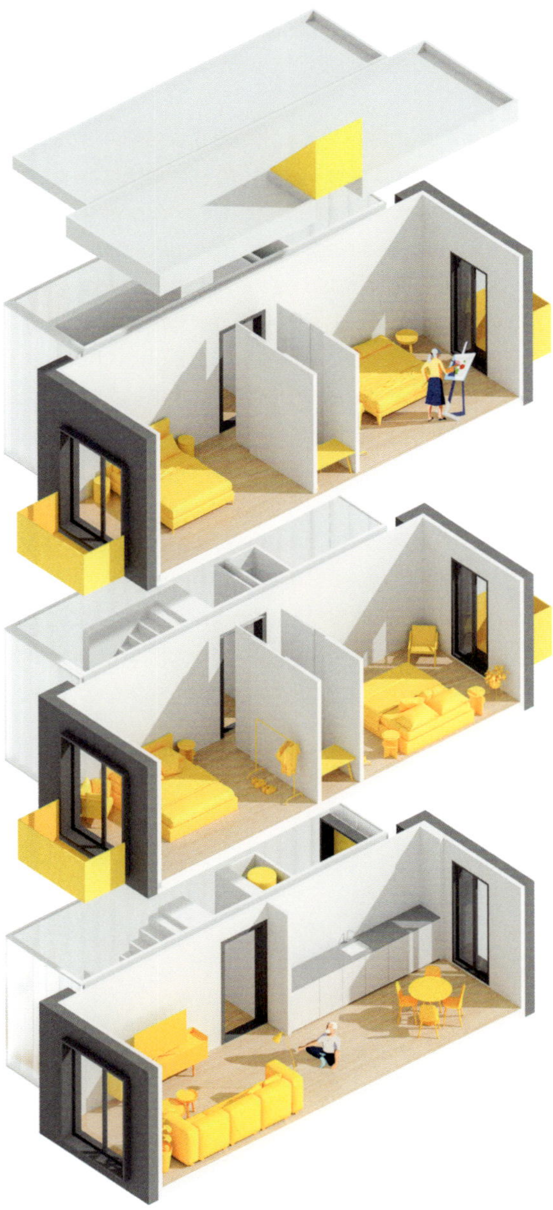

Kit House

Town House, New Islington, 2016

We plan for the numbers to grow rapidly. With quality control and the vertical integration of the supply chain in mind, we bought the manufacturing business, and rechristened it Urban Splash Modular. Our intention is to generate a family of prefabricated housing types: a 'guest' edition, Fab House, which has been customised by George Clarke off the telly working with TDO Architecture; a new mid-rise, single-core, walk-up apartment block concept called Mansion House, made out of CLT (cross-laminated timber); and a smaller designer starter-home typology we're calling Row House to work in more constrained and compact environments while still maximising space, light and height. And we won't be stopping there – we have an ambition to develop semi-detached and potentially detached typologies, too, in due course.

It's a journey we've only just started. So far, we have two market-tested products and we're in the process of making it affordable to the widest possible band of homebuyers. We're driving down the manufacture cost wherever we can, rigorously interrogating, honing and refining every element of production, from foundations and floors to light fittings and door hinges.

It's a practice the volume-builders regard as second nature, and one we must respect; the difference being that, as we shave pennies and pounds off our build cost, we're keeping an iron grip on the quality and space standards we've set ourselves. Every efficiency we sweat over is in the service of putting beautiful, light, spacious, architect-designed homes within reach of a greater number of people, and ultimately displacing dark, cramped, volume-built cookie-cutter homes from the market altogether.

If we've always been passionate about the qualities of the home at the scale of the individual apartment, house or building, our other long-term preoccupation has been the wider neighbourhood. Increasingly now, we are working at this larger scale on area-based regeneration and placemaking.

Factory floor, Urban Splash Modular, 2018

My view of the world is that everything is becoming more and more industrialised and being made more efficiently in factories. Housing is one of the last bastions there is; the UK will either grab hold of modular and get on board or be left behind. We like innovation and we want to be driving that future, building thousands of homes a year as soon as we can.

Tom Bloxham

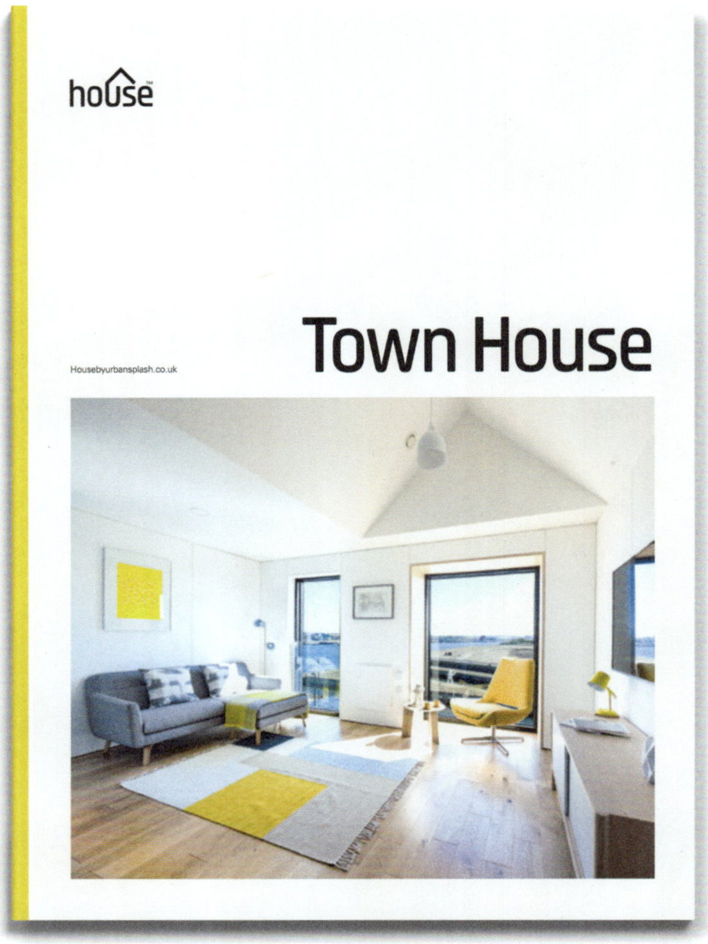

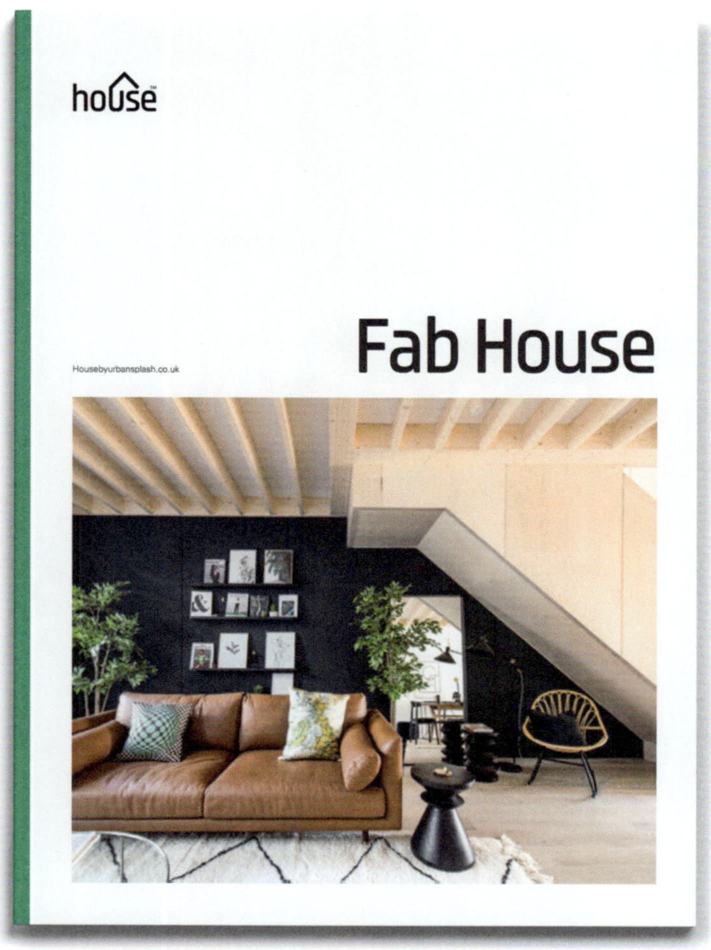

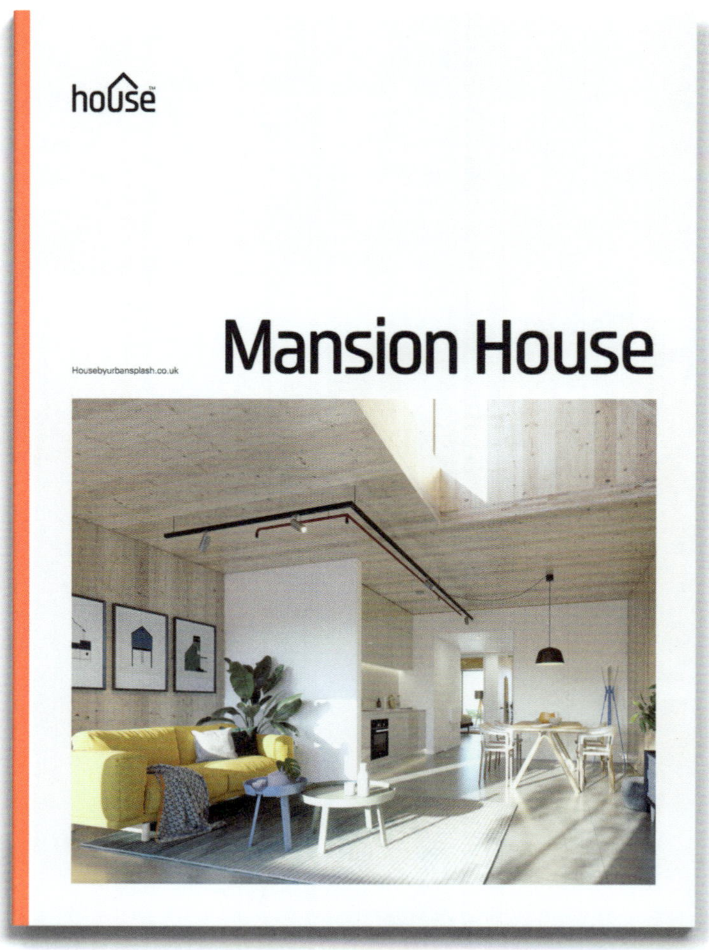

House product brochures, 2018

14
Town House
Inner space.
Space is an incredibly valuable thing. Personal space, living space, breathing space, work space, chill out space. As our lives become more and more complicated, so the desire for a little more space goes up. That's why the first question we ask when designing your house is 'How much space do you want?' The answer's a simple choice between two floors or three, giving you a more-than-generous 1,000 sq ft or 1,500 sq ft, respectively.
With full-height windows and doors, and impressively high ceilings, House maximises natural light and creates a sense of flow between rooms. So not only does House actually have more space, but it makes better use of that space as well. Forget cats – you could swing an elephant in our House.
How much do you want?
Part 01. Design.
15

22
Town House
Future proof.
If there's one thing we've learnt over the years, it's that it's impossible to predict what's coming next. Plans go out of windows, curve balls are thrown and spanners are put in the works. It's not just our circumstances that change, our personalities do too: raucous nights out turn into sensible nights in; house parties with people you've never met turn into dinner parties discussing local OFSTED reports.
Sadly House does not come with its own crystal ball, but it does come with a great deal of flexibility. The outside walls are the only load-bearing ones, so everything else can change as your life does. Spare bedrooms can become home offices; man-caves with impressive sound systems can turn into cosy nurseries. Whatever life throws at you, with House you can change more than a coat of paint.
Flexible layout.
Part 01. Design.
23

Future neighbourhoods
large scale, rich mix, long life.

When we talk about future neighbourhoods we're not ashamed to sound a little evangelical. Society is on the cusp of revolutions in personal transport, modular housing and flexible working – we need a revolution in the design of neighbourhoods, too.

"If people live in houses where do the houses live? If they are homeless all we are left with is the typical endless, featureless suburbia."
Gordon Cullen, Maryculter, 1974

We want people to demand better places to live and work. Homes that they love, that are bigger, lighter, more flexible, more sustainable, cheaper to run, better suited to how we live now and unashamedly modern. Liveable neighbourhoods with more shared space, more green places, fewer cars, more playing out and less sitting in. We think it will happen, it's a question of how quickly and who will lead us there.

It's also a question of how. We don't underestimate the complex challenges of bringing forward large-scale, long-term, multi-phase area-wide projects. It requires vision, tenacity, adaptability to circumstance, a willingness to think on a grand scale but also to listen to the hopes and concerns of individuals.

The recent examples of outstanding new build schemes that do exist, such as the Stirling Prize-winning Accordia scheme or Great Kneighton, both in Cambridge, demonstrate that what's required is a commitment to quality at every level, from the layout and planning of streetscapes to the design and configuration of homes, to plantings, windows, railings and door handles. Every element must convey the same care and attention to detail, as well as a tangible relationship to a clear, overall vision.

"Always design a thing by considering it in its next largest context – a chair in a room, a room in a house, a house in an environment, an environment in a city plan."
Eero Saarinen

Smith's Dock masterplan, North Shields, 2018

It's imperative that we learn from the UK's rich experience of planning new communities. Developers should be – and we are – extracting wisdom from successful examples, such as New Lanark, Bournville, Saltaire and Port Sunlight (all built to house factory workers, between the 1780s and 1900), and more recent, larger-scale schemes such as the postwar new towns. We need to heed the lesson of investing in rich mixtures of high-quality architecture, tenure and public space, and in creating ecologies of uses that generate long-term employment and social interaction. We need to strike up the public-private partnerships and financing structures that can sustain these long-term visions.

We have learned a lot from our work on New Islington in Manchester. It has not been plain sailing by any means but the transformation of this area from one of Manchester's most neglected and run-down neighbourhoods into a striking and satisfying new place to live is one of the most exciting projects we've ever undertaken.

We can now combine our skills in managing complex, multi-phase, large-scale mixed-use regeneration projects and placemaking with a growing housebuilding capacity to bring a new set of opportunities to the market.

As we move towards our fourth decade as a regeneration business, what motivates us is much the same as when we started out in the 1990s. We may be older and more experienced but we are no more comfortable or content with the obvious, the tried-and-tested, the mediocre or the formulaic. Being told "it will never work" is still a call to action rather than a discouragement. We continue to thirst for different and better ways to do things, to pioneer and improve. We may be established, but we remain innovators.

And there is still much regeneration work to be done. Core city centres have been steadily recovering but the national housing system is broken and many people and places continue to be left behind.

The need for unconventional thinking and, even more importantly, action to break the deadlocks in the housing system remains as deep as ever. The Urban Splash record is one of refusing to accept received wisdom and tired formulas; of coming at problems from unusual angles, introducing new solutions, and finding the means to make them work.

A deep recession has reminded us of what is important, getting back to our original benchmark of "would I live there" and staying true to a vision – brand and values matter. We are on a mission. We want to deliver exceptional places for people to live and work, and better futures for our towns and cities.

Back in 1995, the sales brochure for Urban Splash's second major project – Smithfield Buildings in Manchester's now established Northern Quarter – set out a bold aspiration which has become an unofficial rallying cry ever since. It remains as powerful a motivation to us today as it ever was:

We will leave this city not less but greater, better and more beautiful than it was left to us.

Oath of allegiance sworn by the citizens of ancient Athens

The future

Port Loop
Birmingham

Residential / Commercial / Leisure
Architects: Maccreanor Lavington / shedkm / Glenn Howells Architects / Grant Associates

Most developments start with a spreadsheet not a manifesto. Sometimes it is necessary to step back and evaluate what we are trying to achieve, not just a great place to live but a transformative place. We should try to learn from successful neighbourhoods elsewhere and put new ideas into practice, we need to understand why Dutch kids are the happiest in the world or why Japanese towns are the safest. We need not just to respond to how we live now but anticipate change and encourage change.

Jonathan Falkingham

Manifesto for a future neighbourhood, 2017

02. PLAY OUT 'TIL TEA
WE WANT OUR KIDS TO PLAY OUT & WE WANT TO PLAY OUT TOO
AN ISLAND'S BOUNDARIES AFFORD A KIND OF SAFE HAVEN FOR ADVENTURE, WHERE GREATER FREEDOM COMES FROM CONTAINMENT AND WHERE ISLAND RULES CAN ENCOURAGE FREE-RANGING FAMILY LIFE
PORT LOOP OUTDOOR SYSTEM
MORE FUN OUTDOORS
NO BALL GAMES
MORE VITAMIN D
CULTIVATING AN OUTDOOR OUTLOOK
PLAY WITHOUT DIGITAL
EVERYDAY ROUTINES

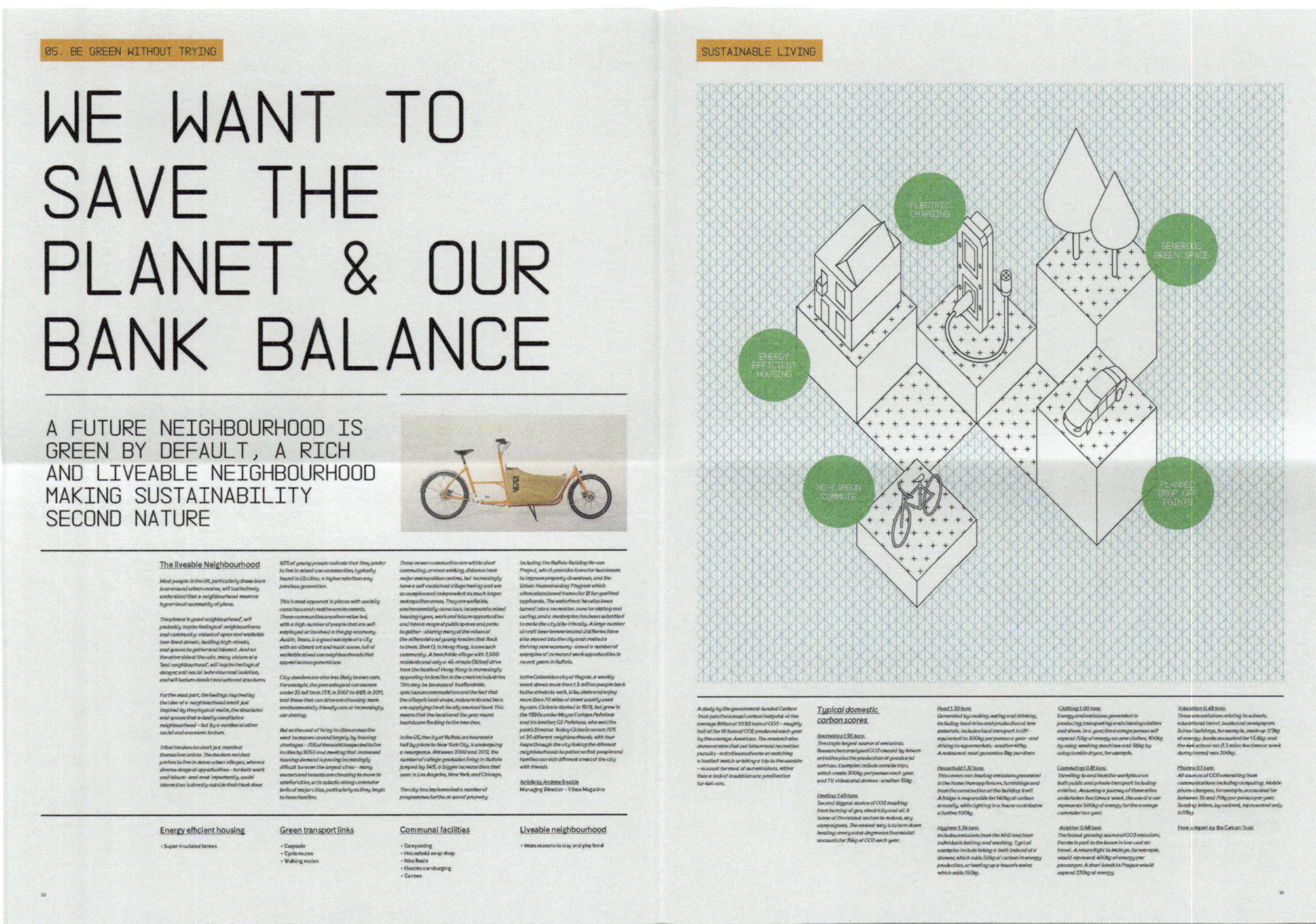
05. BE GREEN WITHOUT TRYING
WE WANT TO SAVE THE PLANET & OUR BANK BALANCE
A FUTURE NEIGHBOURHOOD IS GREEN BY DEFAULT, A RICH AND LIVEABLE NEIGHBOURHOOD MAKING SUSTAINABILITY SECOND NATURE
SUSTAINABLE LIVING

Campbell Park North
Milton Keynes

Residential / Commercial / Leisure
Architects: Metropolitan Workshop / shedkm / Glenn Howells Architects / Grant Associates

The original Plan for Milton Keynes is a fascinating read, it shows the absolute commitment to providing access to quality housing for all, with well-being at its core, delivered by the state.

We think our challenge is to recapture the ethos of the original plan, above all the democracy of access to quality housing, using whatever tools we can, new housing formats, new models of tenure. Milton Keynes was planning for the future, we need to invoke that spirit. We've been known to get a bit soap boxy about it!

Jonathan Falkingham

The Plan for Campbell Park North, 2017

06
Context
Make no little plans, they have no magic to stir men's blood
Daniel Hudson Burnhame
Introduction
We share the enthusiasm of the many who hold the founding principles dear and argue for the continuation of the 'grand plan'. We also understand the need to meet the modern challenges of social, environmental and technological change. We believe it is necessary to fully understand the founding principles, to carefully critique the interceding decades and then to look boldly ahead in the pioneering spirit of the original.
We do not see apparently competing pressures as irreconcilable. The need for greater density does not necessarily mean a move away from the new town or garden city ideal. Far from eroding the logic of gridroads and redways, these provide unique opportunities for embracing new technologies and encouraging lower car dependency. Creating new mixed tenure, intergenerational and liveable neighbourhoods is a continuation of the Milton Keynes ethos and story.
Our aim would be to deliver a truly exceptional place to live (and work) that adds to the cultural and social life of the city and takes the new town ideal onto the next level. In considering the defining principles for our proposal we have revisited the six stated goals of the MKDC Plan for Milton Keynes 1970 and projected these forward.

44
The Plan for Campbell Park North
A place for all: sustainable and liveable neighbourhood
Our aim for Campbell Park North is to provide a mix of housing types and tenures for an inclusive neighbourhood.
Balance and variety are the hallmarks of successful cities. Milton Keynes was founded with an appetite for equality – a place for all: young and old, for different-sized families and different financial outlooks; for bright minds and strong communities. Campbell Park North will bring houses and apartments, co-working and home-working; places to work, play, live and grow – through mixed typologies and tenures, multi-generational and liveable neighbourhoods.
Mixed typologies
One Bed 27%
Two Bed 30%
Two Bed + 19%
Three Bed 14%
Four bed 6%
Live-work 4%
From one-bedroom apartments to family homes: private gardens and village greens, Campbell Park North welcomes people of all ages, ethnicity and income. With an array of choice in size, style and type, our plans factor in the changes and challenges of our time to create a neighbourhood where residents can scale up and down, adapt and change, whilst remaining part of a vibrant, cohesive community.
45
Mixed tenures
Owner occupier 50%
Shared 30%
PRS 10%
Retirement Living 10%
As with the city's original ethos, we will continue a tradition of building strong communities through mixed tenure: of homes for rent and for sale: affordable and secure. Mixed tenures offer residents mobility and flexibility, sharing the success of the UK's fastest-growing city, and breaking down barriers to success and wellbeing.
Multi-generational neighbourhoods
Single 24%
Couple 31%
Family 22%
Multi-gen 13%
Retirement 10%
Milton Keynes' original vision created a place for family life: a safe, supportive city environment with places for kids to play and families to grow. Building on those egalitarian ideals and social goals, Campbell Park North is for both young people and old, somewhere that support carers and careers, and is inclusive and innovative. This is a neighbourhood designed to meet the needs of its residents, helping people from different backgrounds and walks of life thrive.
Liveable neighbourhoods
Work 25%
Co-work 10%
Recreation 1 5%
Health 15%
Community 35%
Fred Roche and the MKDC team recognised 'the duty of architecture to improve society'. Campbell Park North's fresh air and first class facilities are a living, breathing example of those ideals. Denser and greener, it combines the best of the city and the park: a place to walk, run, ride and row. With towpaths and green trails; in a city of some 22 million trees, it is a light, bright, place to call home.

House at Campbell Park North, Milton Keynes

Urban Splash Modular is a game-changer. Other people have tried modular and failed because they haven't put design at the forefront of everything they've sought to do.

George Clarke,
Architect and broadcaster

The first 25 years

400 awards
54 RIBA awards*

*including Housing Design Awards

1993

Project
Concert Square,
Liverpool
Urban Splash Architects / Shed

6 Awards
2 RIBA Awards

1994

Project
Schoolhouse,
Manchester
Urban Splash Architects

2 Awards
1 RIBA Award

2000

Project
New Islington,
Manchester
SMC Alsop / shedkm / dMFK / Stephenson Bell / Grant Associates / FAT / Mae

25 Awards
4 RIBA Awards

2001

Project
Box Works,
Manchester
Urban Splash Architects

12 Awards
2 RIBA Awards

2002

Project
Timber Wharf,
Manchester
Glenn Howells Architects

10 Awards
3 RIBA Awards

2003

Project
Budenburg Haus Projekte,
Altrincham
Foster + Partners /
Urban Splash Architects

25 Awards
4 RIBA Awards

2004

Project
Lister Mills,
Bradford
Latham Architects / shedkm /
David Morley Architects

10 Awards

2010

Project
Matchbox,
Liverpool
shedkm

2 Awards

2011

Project
Lakeshore,
Bristol
Ferguson Mann Architects

16 Awards
3 RIBA Awards

2012

Project
Saxton,
Leeds
Union North

11 Awards
3 RIBA Awards

2013

Project
Park Hill,
Sheffield
Studio Egret West / Hawkins Brown / Mikhail Riches /
Grant Associates /

15 Awards
4 RIBA Awards

2014

Project
Royal William Yard,
Plymouth
Ferguson Mann Architects /
Gillespie Yunnie Architects

35 Awards
7 RIBA Awards

1995

Project
Smithfield Buildings,
Manchester
Stephenson Bell

11 Awards
4 RIBA Awards

1996

Project
Britannia Mills,
Manchester
Urban Splash Architects

7 Awards
1 RIBA Award

1997

Project
Collegiate,
Liverpool
shedkm

5 Awards
2 RIBA Awards

1998

Project
Tea Factory,
Liverpool
Urban Splash Architects /
shedkm

5 Awards
1 RIBA Award

1999

Project
Matchworks,
Liverpool
shedkm

4 Awards
1 RIBA Award

2005

Project
3Towers,
Manchester
Union North

5 Awards
1 RIBA Award

2006

Project
Chimney Pot Park,
Salford
shedkm

17 Awards
3 RIBA Awards

2007

Project
Rotunda,
Birmingham
Glenn Howells Architects

7 Awards

2008

Project
Fort Dunlop,
Birmingham
shedkm

25 Awards
1 RIBA Award

2009

Project
Midland Hotel,
Morecambe
Union North

8 Awards
2 RIBA Awards

2015

Project
House,
New Islington, Irwell Riverside,
Manchester
shedkm

16 Awards
1 RIBA Award

2016

Project
Stubbs Mill,
New Islington,
Manchester
Sixtwo Architects

3 Awards
1 RIBA Award

2017

Project
Smith's Dock,
North Shields
shedkm / SimpsonHaugh /
Fabrik / George Clarke /
TDO Architecture

2 Awards
1 RIBA Award

2018

Project
Avro,
Manchester
Stephenson STUDIO

It Will Never Work
Past Presidents RIBA exhibition quotes

Past President 2003 – 2005
George Ferguson CBE PPRIBA
Mayor of Bristol 2012–16 | People and Cities

Of course, it will never work.

A couple of mad-hat dreamers building a mould-breaking design-led property empire, ignoring all good advice from surveyors and agents? What a farcical notion that they can change the way we live in our cities by gutting and stuffing old industrial buildings and sites that no-one else would touch – and in our challenged Northern cities too.

If anything makes one believe in the art of the impossible it is the improbable story of these two rock stars of urban regeneration who then had the cheek to invade the South! It has been a roller-coaster 25 years of high design, demonstrating that dogged determination, and wild imagination, combined with some of the best architecture in the UK, is a very potent mix – but of course it will never work!

Past President 2005 – 2007
Jack Pringle PPRIBA
Principal, EMEA Regional Director, Perkins+Will

I hadn't really paid much attention to Urban Splash until my run up to be RIBA president in 2005–7 and then they seemed to be everywhere. In my two years in office they won nearly 100 awards, using great architects in low value areas. Surely that can't work? And for such hyper cool lads from the North they seem to be very supportive of the RIBA. They were everywhere, at every party and at every after party. There were paradoxes all around. So, what was the trick?

The "trick" was and is a great partnership, a visionary partnership, between Tom Bloxham, a natural and serial entrepreneur and Jonathan Falkingham, an architect who can see which way is up. They built their business from the ground up and didn't let early set-backs deter them. With huge energy and foresight they bought properties for "less than the price of a carpet" and instead of demolishing them as others would have – they turned them into cool lofts and workplaces, establishing a superb company. They may be twenty-five years old, but they were always ten years ahead of the curve. Their use of top architects, because only they could get the best out of challenging low-budget projects, has been very shrewd.

Urban Splash or Urban Legend? Here's to the next 25.

Past President 2007 – 2009
Sunand Prasad PPRIBA
Senior Partner – Penoyre & Prasad

However much you believe in the power of architecture and design to transform places there is always a slight sense of disbelief when someone actually goes and does it. And Urban Splash have gone and done it at industrial scale. Again and again for 25 years! Bloody-mindedly picking the most unpromising, most decayed land and buildings, abandoned by all the know-alls; then with wild confidence turning it into humming urbanity full of people, energy and life.

Urban Splash seem to transmit through the complex arts of development, the unique spirit of late 80's Manchester, as technically proficient as stylish, brave and infectious.

Past President 2009 – 2011
Ruth Reed HonAIA FRIAS PPRIBA
Green Planning Studio Ltd

The joy of Urban Splash is how contagious their confidence is. In cities across England, they have found the buildings that are key to the identity of the place and imbued them with new life and vision, shouting out to the community that it is worth investing in, raising public confidence.

The Urban Splash development that is closest to my heart I have known both before and after its regeneration. Park Hill Sheffield was a no-go area in the 70's and 80's when I lived in the city. What should have been a monument to social housing was an oppressive reminder of lack of investment and poor management hanging over the city centre. Taking huge but very successful liberties with the fabric of this listed building it now sparkles back, radiating new confidence.

The role that good design has played in this and the other schemes they have been responsible for has provided exemplars for the role great design plays in regeneration. For Park Hill and many other acts of faith in investing in challenging but important buildings, I am really glad that they did make it work.

Past President 2011 – 2013
Angela Brady OBE PDSA PPRIBA
Brady Mallalieu Architects

Open the Urban Splash website and you will read – About Us: "In the beginning, there was no big plan, no strategy, just a wholehearted belief in cities, in design, in architecture and a desire to make things better".

When Tom and Jonathan got together twenty-five years ago they fused a great energy to create something from nothing – decaying sheds of a bygone age were transformed into desirable loft apartments and cool trendy workspaces, from Manchester and Liverpool to Sheffield and beyond. I remember visiting some of their projects on our English Heritage Urban Panel visits and being amazed by their casual business creativity and tremendous success at creating innovative places, that were a joy to visit and recommend to others as exemplar projects. They were the cool boys up North bringing vast old stone mills and warehouses back into urban everyday life.

Good design was always top of their agenda, rewarding them with business success over the years. They have won over 40 RIBA awards for their creative excellence. They make regeneration fun and sustainably the right thing to do, from the largest listed structure in Europe at the iconic Park Hill regenerated estate in Sheffield, to the hands on approach by home buyers getting involved in planning their own new House project, as in New Islington, Manchester.

Urban Splash is About 'US'. Where they feel they 'would like to live and want to work', a great work ethos with still many more projects to come. Their well selected name says it all – a Splash of Urban delight.

Past President 2013 – 2015
Stephen R Hodder MBE PPRIBA
Chairman, Hodder & Partners

Smithfield Buildings was perhaps the first Urban Splash building I visited (with Kisho Kurokawa) in 1997 and I recall we both applauded what had been achieved. Imagination, good architecture and quality were refreshingly at the forefront of the building's renewal, an approach which seems to have underpinned every Splash development since then. The development pre-empted Lord Rogers' Towards an Urban Renaissance and the case for densification of our cities. It signalled the return to living in Manchester city centre.

However, for me, it is the change it has engendered in the culture of development that is most significant... the story of Urban Splash has not simply been about the developments or architecture. Very often it's work has been with ignored, forgotten, or challenging buildings and environments...bringing an inventiveness to regeneration, whether it be with terraced housing in Salford, or the derelict Fort Dunlop in Birmingham, Park Hill in Sheffield or New Islington in Manchester. Each day I stare out from my office across the Bridgewater Canal at my favourite, Timber Wharf completed in 2002, which represented a step forward in the building technology of inner-city residential development. Sixteen years on, and that same pioneering approach is seeking to redress outmoded construction methodologies with the development of 'House', a prefabricated flexible home.

It is this transformation of the culture of development and the quality of what has been delivered that so many other developers have tried to emulate but never quite matched.

And it all started in Manchester and Liverpool...!

Past President 2015 – 2017
Jane Duncan AIA RIAS PPRIBA
Jane Duncan Architects

Stephen Gardiner's quote comes to mind at once when I think of Urban Splash "Good buildings come from good people, and all problems are solved by good design."

A sneaky peek at the Urban Splash trophy shelf bulging with RIBA Awards surely glows with their energy, excitement and still apparently youthful enthusiasm for breaking the development mould, by brilliantly harnessing the naturally gushing lateral creativity of architects allowed off the leash.

They have been rightly rewarded for having mined the multifarious and often untapped opportunities in developing and restoring under loved buildings around the country, many derelict and listed. They have run towards ideas which others have dumped, and been richly rewarded with accolades for such as diverse projects as Saxton in Leeds, Park Hill in Sheffield, Royal William Yard in Plymouth, the Midland Hotel, Morecambe, Fort Dunlop, Birmingham and many Manchester and Liverpool warehouses.

The UK is a better, more exciting place to live in due to Urban Splash's imaginative business strategies. At the centre of their success is, without doubt, a reliance upon brilliant architects, and the natural result is an unprecedented number of RIBA Awards.

Well done to Tom and Jonathan's team. There's more to come I have no doubt.

President
Ben Derbyshire PRIBA
Chair, HTA Design LLP

There is no better example of how design can add value to the business of development in the built environment than is to be found in the work of Urban Splash. In my view that is because it's founders, entrepreneur Tom Bloxham and architect Jonathan Falkingham, have a proper understanding of what design is.

Their combination of talents demonstrates the impact of critical thinking, the core component of design skill, alongside creativity, communication, and an aesthetic sensibility. If you are going to truly benefit from the input of design talent to your business, you need to permit its influence from the very beginning, and across the full range of your process.

From the moment I first came across Urban Splash, I could see that was the case. Everything they do is informed and improved by good design. The result, from humble beginnings, is an enviable oeuvre in master-planning, the architecture of new and refurbished buildings, regeneration and placemaking. And they have been generous with it, contributing much to the culture of architecture and design, including at the RIBA.

So now they can say, with justification, 'Look on my works, oh ye mighty, and despair!'

It would never have worked without all our collaborators, large or small and all our staff past and present.

In delivering this body of work we are indebted to the army of individuals and companies that have assisted us on all the projects in this book. Regeneration of buildings and places is tricky, by definition the old models have failed and new models are required – doing the same old same old just won't wash. To conceive and implement new models and ideas we have always relied heavily on the brightest and most talented – individuals who think from first principals and challenge received wisdom - whether that is our own in-house staff, the best up and coming designers and architects or the project partners who have shared our passion and vision to deliver new solutions and new neighbourhoods.

Jonathan Falkingham

Partners

Advantage West Midlands
Birmingham Alliance
Birmingham City Council
Bradford Metropolitan District Council
Bristol City Council
Canal & River Trust
Central Manchester Development Corporation
City Challenge
County and City of Swansea
Creative Sheffield
English Heritage
English Partnerships
European Regional Development Fund
Great Places Housing Group
Hammerson plc
Heritage Lottery Fund
Historic England
HM Treasury
Homes & Communities Agency
Homes England
Invest in Bradfrord
Irvine Bay Urban Regeneration Company
Irwell Valley Housing Association
Lancaster City Council
Leeds City Council
Liverpool City Council
Liverpool Land Development Company
Liverpool Vision
Manchester City Council
Manchester Methodist Housing Association
Maritime Housing Association
Mendip District Council
Ministry of Housing, Communities & Local Government
New East Manchester
New Islington Free School
North Ayrshire Council
North Liverpool Partnership
North Somerset Council
North Tyneside Council
North West Regional Development Agency
One North East
Peel Holdings PLC
Places for People
Plymouth City Council
Re'new
RopeWalks Partnership
Salford City Council
Seedley and Langworthy Partnership
Sheffield City Council
South West Regional Development Agency
Speke Garston Development Co.
Stockton Borough Council
Tameside Metropolitan Borough Council
Tees Valley Regeneration
The Housing Corporation
The William Pears Group
Town Centre Securities
Trafford Metropolitan Borough Council
Trafford Park Development Corporation
Transform South Yorkshire
Walsall Metropolitan Borough Council
Walsall Regeneration Company
Warrington Borough Council
Welsh Assembley Government
West Somerset Council
Yorkshire Forward

Architects

Adjaye Associates
Alford Hall Monaghan Morris
Alison Brooks Architects
Arkheion
Austin-Smith:Lord
BDP
Ben Kelly Design
David Morley Architects
De Metz Forbes Knight
Design Studio
dMFK Architects
DSDHA
Fabrik
FAT
Feix & Merlin
Ferguson Mann
Fielden Clegg Bradley
Flacq
Foster + Partners
Future Systems
Gareth Hoskins
George Clarke
Gillespie Yunnie
Glenn Howells
Grant Associates
Gross Max Landscape
Hawkins\Brown
Ian Simpson Architects
Ice Architects
Kinetic
Latham Architects
Levitate Architecture
Mae
Make
Matthew Heywood
Maurice Shapero
Mikhail Riches
NORD
Planit
Project Orange
Q2
Querkraft
R2 Architects
Re-Form Landscape
Reiach & Hall Architects
Richard Rogers Partnership
Riches Hawley Mikhail
Ryder Architecture
shedkm
SimpsonHaugh
Sixtwo Architects
SMC Alsop
Snook
Space Craft
Stephenson Bell
Stephenson STUDIO
Studio 3
Studio Egret West
TDO Architecture
Union North
Weston Williamson

Creatives

Adrian Burrows
AM Design & Creative
Andy Brown
Assembly Studios
B&W
BB Saunders
Ben Blackall
Boom Creative
Bristol Records Office
Charlotte Wood Photography
Core Marketing
Cubed Thinking
Dalton Maag
Daniel Hopkinson
Darc Studio
Designers Republic
Dom Moore
Duerden Collection
Ear to the Ground
Elevator Creative
Emma Benyon
Extravision
Falconer Associates
Felix Mooneeram
Finn PR
Go
Guy Harris
Haarkon
Hugh Burden
Human
Iron Bird
Jane Field Stylist
Jason Lock
Jennifer Newman Studio
Joe Coleman
Joel Chester Fildes
Jon Hatton
Jonathan Keenan
Jonathan Moore Photography
JP74
Karen Wright
Kate Amin
Len Grant
Loft Interiors
Love Creative
Luke Unsworth
Magnetic North
Marketing Manchester
Martin Crombie
McCoy Wynne Associates
Media Rose Michelle Collier
MK Public Relations
Modern Designers
Morley Von Sternberg
Mutant Labs
Nest.co.uk
Nic Gaunt
Nick Hufton
No Chintz
North
Ocean Studios
Onshore
Patrick Young
Paul Groom
People Will Always Need Plates
Peter & Paul
Peter Bennett Photography
Phil Griffin
Plaster
Price & Myers
Richard Cooper, Photoflex
Richard Downer
Robert Whitrow
Shaw + Shaw
ShedID
Simon Griffin
Simon Webb
Slant Media
Smiling Wolf
Smooth
Spoken-Image
Squint/Opera
Studio Treble
The Anderson Small Associates
The Neighbourhood
The Warehouse Project
Tim Sinclair
Tim Smith
Tokyo Wolf
Tom Benn
Trevor Burrows
Trevor Johnson
Uniform
United Creatives
Utility
Very Creative
Village Screen
Vox Multimedia
Warehouse Home
Yap Films

Consultants

Adams Kara Taylor
AECOM
Align Building Control
Artez
Ashmount Consulting Engineers
Atelier Ten
Baker Hollingworth
Baker Shepherd Gillespie
BDSP
Beechfield Consulting Engineers
Bennett Williams
Bevan Brittan
BLM Law
Booth King Partnership
Broadfield Project Management
Buro Happold
Camlins
Civic
Civic Engineers
Cox Turner Morse
Creative Heritage
Cundalls
Curtins Consulting
Davis Langdon
DBK
dBX Acoustics Ltd
Dewhurst MacFarlane
Elliott Wood Partnership
Eversheds
Fulcrum
Gardiner & Theobald
Gerrard O'Donnell
Gleeds
Gross Max
Gunner Cooke
HCD
Hoare Lea
Hulley & Kirkwood
Identity Consult
JDS
Joule Consultants
Landscape Projects
Lk Group
MACH Acoustics
Malcom Hughes
Mann Williams
Martin Stockley Associates
Max Fordham
Menzies Partners
MFA Building Control
Olsson Fire & Risk
Pannone
Price and Myers
Progressive Service Design
R Vint Engineering
Rawlings Consultancy Services
RBC Limited
Robertson Construction
RPS Group Plc
Salford Archaeological
Salus Approved Inspectors
Service Connections
SIG
Simon Fenton Partnership
Stockley
Structures 1
Syntegra Energy Consulting
TACE Mechanical & Electrical
TD Bingham
Turner and Townsend
Whitby Bird
WRW Group

Funders

English Partnerships
European Regional Development Fund
Greater Manchester Pension Fund
Handelsbanken
Heritage Lottery Fund
Historic England
Homes & Communities Agency
HSBC
ICG-Longbow
Lloyds Bank
North West Regional Development Agency
Places for People
Rothschild & Co
Royal Bank of Scotland
The Co-operative Bank
The William Pears Group
Urban Exposure

Edited by
Miles Falkingham

Foreword by
Deyan Sudjic OBE

Contributions by
Michael Evamy
Mark Latham
Robert Senior
Tom Bloxham MBE
Jonathan Falkingham MBE

Documentary photography
Felix Mooneeram

Archive images
Dom Moore
Getty Images
Guy Harris
Haarkon
Joel Chester Fildes
Jonathan Keenan
Nic Gaunt
Paul Groom
Picture Plane
Richard Cooper / Photoflex
Richard Downer
Shaw + Shaw
Simon Webb
Tim Sinclair
Tom Bird
Uniform
Urban Splash Archive

Designed by
Smiling Wolf

Printed by
Pureprint

ISBN 978-1-9164611-0-9

Contact
Urban Splash Ltd.
Timber Wharf
16–22 Worsley Street
Castlefield
Manchester M15 4LD
0161 839 2999
urbansplash.co.uk

Follow us
twitter.com/urban_splash
facebook.com/urbansplash
instagram.com/weareurbansplash